Negotiate:

RESOLVE IT RIGHT

MARY KENDALL HOPE, PH. D.

Pax Pugna Publishing

Raleigh, North Carolina

Pax Pugna Publishing
An imprint of LuLu Press
3101 Hillsborough Street
Raleigh, North Carolina 27607
ISBN: 978-1-4834-0934-4
Printed in the United States of America

Book Design: Mary Kendall Hope

CONTENTS

DEDICATION

I would like to Dedicate This Book
To my Two Lovely Daughters, Katelyn & Emily
Mama Loves You
And Thanks You for Allowing Me The
Time to Write This
While Doing My First Job
Of Being Your Mother

ACKNOWLEDGMENT

I would like to acknowledge
The fine work of
The professors at Harvard's Program on Negotiation
Who Inspired Me
To Teach and Write About Negotiation

I hope you will
Appreciate this work I have done to help
The General Public
To Understand & Embrace the Skills Needed to
Negotiate

Chapter 1

Defining NEGOTIATION

*Nothing can stop the man
with the right mental attitude
from achieving his goal;
nothing on earth can help the man
with the wrong mental attitude.*

Thomas Jefferson

Negotiation: You Stating *Your* Position

When you **negotiate** you are always stating *your* position in response to a presented conflict.

"A **negotiation** is made of two sides that are *both* stating their separate positions and both trying to get what they want. A negotiation has <u>no</u> third party professional who is specifically hired to be neutral.

Third party neutrals are mediators, facilitators, and arbitrators. I have defined the differences between these practices and professions in chapter five. All of these professions (mediation, facilitation, & arbitration) are based on and utilize good negotiation skills."

To succeed you need first to learn how to negotiate your position well.

Educate yourself: If there are attorney's involved in a negotiation or if there are other professionals, diplomatic representatives or business associates, the objectives are still the same. Both sides are maneuvering through either statements or actions to get what they want.

10 Points to Successful Negotiation: The *Negotiate Strategy*™

1. **Listen**
2. Respectfully **Make A Simple Request**
3. Do not argue. Do not justify your choices. Do not interrupt. **Listen**

4. As you Listen and **Consider What You Are Hearing**:
5. **Seek to Understand & Empathize** with the Other Sides' Perspective

6. Take Time to **Consider What You've Understood** Before Speaking Again
7. **Make Another Positive Statement** or Respectful Request

If the conversation isn't going well, stop and follow steps 8-10 without discussing points. If the conversation is now progressing well, continue slowly. Do not take on too much. Discuss only one point at a time.

8. **End the conversation after 1-3 points** have been successfully established if possible.
9. **Close with statements of respect** and
10. **Thank the other side** for making time to talk with you.

"Your closing words should be something genuine and respectful, no matter what the other side has said. Leave the situation positively. Establishing just one point positively will help the negotiation by giving it some foundation of positive common ground. Belaboring several points poorly will not."

"You can only control your own actions. No matter what the other side does, you will feel better if you do not engage in a negative statement or exchange."

STUCK? Most People become *stuck* right here. The Argument starts and options shut down. Here's a Method that works if you will take the time to think and consider your problem from a different perspective.

With this work I am presenting a new method the *Negotiate Journal*™ for individuals in conflict to use to prepare themselves to resolve any dispute with someone else by learning to generate options.

Generating New Options is the essential component of the *Negotiate* Journal. You have a problem, obviously, because you have not been able to realize any other way to both *understand* your conflict and create options that will work for both sides. The answer is there. You can find it. The options that you will create when you complete the *Negotiate* Journal will empower your client to use the *Negotiate Strategy* with other side.

Chapter two is dedicated to a process called "Finding Your Voice." This is an essential FIRST STEP for every client. When clients learn to let go of "all or nothing" thinking and get in touch with how they really feel holistically about the problem – they empower themselves with the ability to empathize with the other side – thereby laying their own groundwork for success by finding a resolution that will address all aspects of the problem.

Chapter three is dedicated to completing one's *Negotiate Journal*™ which is a method for taking the work completed in "Finding Their Voice" and transferring their feelings into a step by step method for:

1. Understanding of their "side" of the conflict and
2. Developing empathy and understanding of the *other* side's perspective while
3. Subsequently creating a new set of options for the best resolution that address all aspects of the dispute.

The *Negotiate Journal*™ carries you through a very simple set of questions. The answers will take some time to answer if you complete it right. To resolve something complex, you must reserve the time to think about your problem from a holistic point of view – meaning you consider the other side's perspective as well. When you do this, you unlock the closed walls, doors or barriers to succeeding and they will be free to see new options. The new options you will create (when you complete a *Negotiate* Journal) will come from *your* circumstances & will better address your problem.

If you choose to utilize these steps to develop a manipulative strategy, the outcome will be a waste of time.

Ultimately, manipulative strategies fail BOTH sides. If your opponent did this in the past be watchful. It is likely to happen again unless the other side has good reasons to resolve this.

If the relationship <u>must </u>be resolved **well** (ie: parents or spouses…employers who will continue to employee you…) then you must wipe the slate clean on your side and carefully negotiate in good faith with eyes wide open.

Best to let the past stay in the past.

Good Negotiation

I distinguish the term "good" professional negotiator as one that is:

- ❖ Trained and practices the skills, techniques and protocols of professional negotiation.
- ❖ Seeks both a monetary/property agreement as well as
- ❖ To preserve the relationships of those involved as they pertain to the negotiation to *build* bridges not burn them. This professional behavior produces an holistic resolution.

A **holistic resolution** is one that includes a monetary or property objective as well as a resolution of the issues that have damaged or potentially damaged the relationship of those involved. Whether they are able to state it or not, the public has a silent expectation when they hire a professional that they will achieve a holistic resolution.

All Attorneys are negotiators but they are <u>not</u> all trained in the aspects of holistic resolution skill that I write about in this book. In fact, this is new framework I am presenting for the first time. It is built on an older ADR concept called the BATNA (Fisher, Ury, & Patton, 1981-2011). I detail this well-established professional protocol in chapter three. My **Negotiation Journal™** expands the BATNA from the public's perspective. Some attorney's are trained in this older version, and some are not.

You can hire a good attorney or negotiator to assist you, but you will have the best chance of succeeding if you formulate your own *Negotiation Strategy* by taking time to "Find Your Voice" and write/complete a *Negotiation* Journal.

Negotiation: Extracting the Profession from the Field of Law

As the field of dentistry is a part of the profession of medicine, so is it true today that the field of alternative dispute resolution (ADR) *which includes negotiation* is a part of the field of law. Over time, dentistry was separated from the practice of medicine due to the specific needs of patients and specialized training needed for professionals.

The time for the field of negotiation to be extracted from the field of law has been realized in recent decades. Chapters five and six specify a brief orientation of the major professions of ADR and how to work with these professionals. Flip to this section mow if you feel the need to understand a brief history of dispute resolution and how you can use ADR to help you in your dispute.

The Benefits of Hiring An Attorney

Attorneys bring a set of skills that are very necessary in any society. You need a good attorney on your side in a negotiation when the other side has an attorney. Any person (involved in a lawsuit) needs to secure an attorney to go over important documents, statutes and precedents established so that he/she will be prepared with all of the information that will be needed.

Also, the skills a professional attorney *offers* bring a validity and power to a dispute. Sometimes, the power and validity an attorney brings is needed. An attorney's skills of negotiation are just different from the skills to train a good conflict resolution professional today. Attorneys focus on winning your case, but not necessarily on attaining a client a holistic resolution. Attorneys often sacrifice holistic resolutions in order to win the case.

Sometimes, winning your case is the best option. It truly does depend on the consequences of what you have to lose if you do indeed *lose*.

❖ Every problem is not simply a nail that requires a hammer. Winning your case *well* is better for everyone in the long run, but it may require more time, patience and work.

As I stated above, attorneys are trained to win. A sole objective of "winning" and the other side "losing" is not conducive to an agreement that will address all of the aspects of a dispute.

❖ Those aspects you do *not* address are likely to rear their ugly heads in your near future.

Negotiation: With or Without An Attorney

❖ If you want or need to address the deeper aspects of a dispute, the best help you can give yourself is to use the strategies in this book *with* your attorney to help you reach a more holistic resolution.

Remember, the attorney works for *the client*. The client will be the one who has to either live with the outcome or go back to court later because it didn't stand the test of time. As a negotiator, help your client to get to the best resolution by teaching them to write/complete an *Negotiate Journal*™.

A Monetary/Property Agreement Versus a Holistic Resolution

The resolution that an attorney seeks is most often a monetary or property resolution only. The field of law teaches attorneys that law is free from emotion. Resolving human conflicts **holistically** is about resolving conflicting emotional feelings as well.

If you just focus on the money, property or what you want in any dispute - the person you will shortchange the most is *you*. Whether you realize it or not when you seek to truly resolve a conflict you are seeking a holistic resolution. Holistic resolutions resolve the emotional and financial aspects of a problem.

Always Seek Holistic Resolution: The Most Important Journey is Yours & Your Family's

Most individuals are members of a family. Individuals are often parents and have groups of friends that are also involved (even to a small degree) in their conflict. If you focus on the money or property alone and ignore the emotional components of the problem, this will hurt those closest to you. Often those around you need the emotional aspects of the conflict resolved with just as much priority as the financial.

❖ When you resolve conflicts holistically give yourself the opportunity for making *right* what is wrong from a human standpoint. This frees you to heal and transform your situation and eventually transcend it.

No, it is never *all* your fault. You should not accept all of the blame, but rather accept your part of it.

It is also not all *your* responsibility to formulate a *Negotiation Strategy*. It is the responsibility of the other side as well, but the only person you can change is you.

BAD Negotiation

Bad negotiation skills include:

- Threats,
- Angry statements,
- Demands,
- Writings,
- Propaganda,

- Actions, or
- Violence.

These forms of negotiation run rampant on our news programs, movies, TV shows, video games, and in real life. You don't need a book to help you use that form of negotiation. You simply open your mouth and shout, demand, threaten.... or use violent actions. As professionals we know, these are easy-to-do, but never succeed in truly resolving a conflict so that the people involved learn, grow and prosper.

People fail at negotiation because they do not stop and consider the entire problem. They only consider their perspective and they negate the other perspective. This is a recipe for disaster.

Negotiate: Use Your New Skills In Every Interaction

⇒ When you think **"I am right"** and the other person is simply **"wrong" you will fail** at a negotiation and ultimately fail within the circumstances that surround that negotiation. For instance, a bad set of negotiation skills on a job can ultimately lead you to lose that job.

⇒ Considering other people's feelings and perspective is the first step toward a good resolution, and if you build on an existing resolution with *another* successful resolution to the next conflict - it will lead to more success at that job, and can help you turn around a bad behavior pattern of "I'm right" and "You're Wrong."

It is easy to fall back into old bad ways of negotiation, especially when one sees fictional movie characters and real people using bad negotiation skills. No matter what you used to think about negotiation, here is an essential truth I learned from working with thousands of people in conflict over decades of time.

❖ **If you practice resolving your dispute well**, you will not only experience physical success in the moment, you will also *benefit much more* down the road if you **heal and make your life better because of what you've been through.**

Preparing to Negotiate – The Process *Before* the Statements & Deeds

Another truth I know is that negotiating *well* is -**when you begin to do it well, it becomes how you respond in other areas of your life.** It becomes how you speak and how you act. If one speaks and acts with disrespect, they will get disrespect in return from those they talk to. They will also worsen the conflict. Here's my adaptation of an old adage as it pertains to negotiation:

1. What one *thinks* becomes what one *says.*
2. What one *says* becomes what one *does.*
3. What one *does* becomes *habit* over time.

4. *Negative Habits Never Changed Make up a Life Choice.*
5. Habits Changed Positively, Change *Your* World Positively
6. All of the People in *Your* World will be affected by your habits either positively or negatively.

7. Choose Your Thoughts, Statements and Actions Wisely and with the Consideration of *All* Those Around You.

Negotiating well is a process that begins *first* by understanding the *origins* of the conflict then *changing* the state of what isn't working.

Learning to NEGOTIATE Well – *Negotiator Understand Thyself*

Every interaction in life is a negotiation. Consider the following examples for yourself in *your own* life:

Before we *ever* begin negotiating with family members, co-workers, bosses, authority figures, service people, salesmen.... we first negotiate with ourselves. We negotiate every word that will come out of our mouths and we negotiate every thought.

We negotiate with ourselves every single morning when we wake. Get up now? Wait and sleep a few more minutes?

We weigh the benefits and costs of all of our options and make our choices. Leave early? Wait until I have to? Did you realize that you were negotiating with yourself? Maybe you did.

❖ **Recognition** and **Understanding** of your ability to stop and reason with yourself is important. You can build on this ability by improving every time you do the same action again. This is how Michael Jordon became a star basketball player or any professional athlete became good at what he or she learned to do. *Practice.*

Recognize Your Own Negotiation Skills & Thoughts

Here's an example of how to build this skill. This is how you would build your ability to get up earlier: This may seem simple – but it is a good comparison to the same type of forethought that the skills to negotiate require.

EXAMPLE ONE – *Getting Up*

1. **Start by considering the simple choices you make *before* your action** (*How early do I need to get up?*)**.**
   Let's say every evening when you go to bed you consider:

2. What time you will get up the next morning?
3. Should you go to bed a little early so you can get a little more sleep?
4. How will you fall asleep earlier?

5. Will you work out a little harder to make your body a little more tired?
6. Will you need another type of alarm to help get up?
7. Getting up earlier will make for a less stressful morning and commute to work.
8. **Is this worth it?**

These are all questions to stop and ask yourself. After you've done it once, it becomes easy to fly through the routine of preparing for bed and getting up in the future.

By asking yourself these questions and answering honestly, you are laying the groundwork for a good negotiation with yourself. You can do this about any single area of your life and no matter how long it takes to successfully complete your goal, when you do not make it, you'll still feel better about yourself because inside, you'll know you did the work you needed to – you thought about it. You considered honestly your strength and weaknesses and you're on the right path to succeed if you stick with it after you fail and try again.

❖ If you didn't answer any of the questions honestly – you'll very soon know it.
❖ You'll simultaneously realize the need to go back and be **brutally honest** with yourself.

When you're really honest with yourself – you're free to succeed.

❖ **"Faking good"** only wastes time.

Let's put the "getting up" in the morning example into: a simple *problem* to negotiate:

EXAMPLE TWO – *Making Love*

1. **Start by considering the step by step choices you make *before* your action** (*Will I make love with my spouse tonight?*).
   Let's say every evening when leave work you consider:

2. Will I Spend Intimate Time with My Spouse Tonight?
3. Should I go home a little early to shower/change/ let my spouse know?
4. How can *I* make this experience more interesting and successful?

5. Will I need to do something special or arrange dinner out?

15

6. Will I need to get a babysitter or talk to my spouse about a new idea I have about this?
7. Spending more intimate time with my spouse will help everything about our relationship.
8. **Is this worth it?**

A good negotiation is like painting a house, making a wonderful dinner or making love – the delight one enjoys afterward depends on the *right* preparation.

You at Your Best

As I presented at the beginning, in a negotiation *you* are stating *your* position. Make your presentation its best by **presenting the best you can determine**.

⇒ Ignore those who will call this **"touchy feely."** Others are just jealous because they'd like to have some of that courage that it takes to achieve wisdom. This is basic but true.

Show The *Other Side* Your Best: "When you present yourself at your best – you help everyone else involved in the conflict, including children, loved ones and friends."

⇒ "Others around you always experience the consequences of your actions, as you experience the consequences of others' actions. "

If you are a parent: You want your children to be proud of you and more importantly, you need to be proud of your own ability to resolve things well.

⇒ If you've goofed in the past, it is a waste of time to beat yourself up over failure. Better to focus on doing it again the right way. Those who truly care about you will be glad you did.

The Power of *Optimizing* Everyone Wins, Especially *You*

Never underestimate the power that your positive work will *have* over your conflict when you do your *Negotiate Journal*™ *well*.

"The other side is watching. Whether they show you that they respect you or not, they will *eventually* respect you and show you that they do.

If you continue to persevere and show *them* respect – no matter what you get thrown at you – the other side **will** begin to change."

⇒ "It may take longer than you need or want for the other side to respect you, but trust me, you will make a good impression."

⇒ **"Respect the other side genuinely.** This **will** help the situation."

Seek the holistic resolution that I outline when I describe the *Negotiate Strategy*™ and watch the entire conflict begin to change for the better.

❖ **"The other side will test and try you. They will show you their *worst* just before they are ready to *change* and show you respect."** I emphasize this strongly to clients because I have seen it happen in conflicts so many times when *I* have been the professional assisting people to resolve a conflict.

I also emphasize this because it is so important. The ability to **recognize that the other side is testing you** helps you to stop yourself from sinking back into arguments.

"You must **be patient until the other side shows you respect.** Even if it takes a long time, it will be worth it. They will *eventually* recognize your respect and they *will* respect you back if you remain positive."

This is *often* the difference between success and failure.

Objectives of This Book

This book will only touch on **one** aspect of the steps of negotiation – the one that is required of you as a professional t*o you to prepare for the ambiguous, emotional aspects of the dispute/conflict.*

The other skills of professional negotiation are best left to professionals. This aspect of negotiation is important enough alone to focus on because little to nothing exists (as of the writing of this book) to help professional negotiators prepare clients – to deal with the emotional aspects of conflict.

This *Negotiation Strategy*™ can help any person in conflict.

The information in this book will help you before they get into a room again with the person or persons you are in conflict with. The things you will need to do are *not* easy, but if you take the time and go through the steps I've outlined you will know that you did all you could do to reach resolution.

The final two chapters of this book provide advisement for individuals in personal conflicts and business conflicts. You may or may not have conflicts in these areas right now in your life. These guides are provided for you when you do. Having conflicts with other human beings is so commonplace that we all have to whip our a *Negotiate Journal* from time to time to work out the kinks.

Some of the material in the latter chapters of the book are reviewed from prior sections and repeated where appropriate so that sections of this book may to be utilized as a step-by-step guide to addressing the specific issues in the business setting and in personal situations. The "Finding Your Voice" section is included only once in the next chapter.

Got Options?

One of the biggest pitfalls to success that exists in the popular culture is "ALL or NOTHING" thinking. **If "nothing" is an option, you're not negotiating** you're capitulating & simultaneously losing your opportunity for a real resolution.

Chapter 2

Strike "All or Nothing" Thinking:
Find Your Voice in the Middle

In the long run, we shape our lives,
and we shape ourselves.
The process never ends until we die.
And the choices we make are ultimately
our own responsibility.

Eleanor Roosevelt

Just Because People Say it....

It's "all or nothing." This is a common statement of thinking about resolving a conflict. Let me ask you something, if an entire herd of pigs decide to run over a cliff, does it make it the right thing to do? That analogy comes straight from the Holy Bible (Mark 5:13).

The pigs in this story are infected with "evil spirits" that were cast out of someone close to them. When the evil infects them, they run right off a cliff. One of the lessons of this story is that when one thinks only as the "herd" thinks, one would follow a herd no matter what the herd is doing. Personally, I'd rather be the pig that was smart enough to stop and deal with the problem. How about you?

Here are some questions I'd like you to consider:

1.   **Why strike "all or nothing: Thinking?**

Because "all or nothing" ultimately leaves you with nothing.

❖ If you are lucky enough to get "all" of what you want- then stop and think. Does what you wanted include robbing yourself of truly resolving your problem? If you are really honest with yourself, the answer to that question is No, because you lost something you may never be fortunate enough to get back – relationships and respect.

"Even if you now hate the *other person or side* you were in conflict with – you will lose not only this relationship but also the respect of others around you who wanted and needed you to resolve this well. When enough time passes you will realize that you want and need others to respect you whether your win or lose."

2. Does what you wanted include robbing the other side completely?

Are you really that self-centered? Probably not. Likely there was a time that you thought it was the only way to resolve the situation. Now you know better.

3. Is the "other side" that convinced that they are right?

Probably not, and even if they state that they *are* in public, the real truth is every person and side would like it better if they resolved the conflict well. Sometimes, individuals get caught up in the fight itself. The fight itself becomes a third "player" in your interactions that can take over your thinking and paralyze you.

4. If *you* were one hundred percent right about this issue of conflict would that end the conflict?

No. Others would disagree with you about the same issue. The opposite points of view (to yours) would simply reveal themselves. There are good reasons for the other point of view. Deep down, you realize this. If this were not true, there wouldn't be a conflict.

LET'S SAY YOU "Win" ALL of What You Want

❖ Beyond the moment you feel that you "won" you will very soon begin to feel the loss of your *own* self-respect. You will lose caring from others, and shared experience of resolving this conflict well.

20

Approach a Conflict with Some New Knowledge

1. Why is This Situation a Conflict? Why Isn't it Easy to Fix?

If you are in the middle of a heated conflict – by definition – it is something that has *not* been dealt with before in the manner in which you are experiencing it now. If there were a simple answer out there – you would have already utilized it.

2. How Does Negotiation Help You Find a New Beginning?

A conflict can exist for either a short time or have a long history. A negotiation creates an entirely different atmosphere and approach to this conflict, stimulating you to find a new way of thinking about it. Negotiation is based on some simple but vital truths that in the heat of battle, those involved nearly always forget:

In Every Conflict

❖ **Both sides have something to LOSE** that is going to cause them potential **pain or loss.**

❖ **Both also have something to GAIN** by negotiating a resolution **that combines both sides' perspective**

If you remember these two truths in the *worst* part of the negotiation, it will help you to take a deep breath; be your best, and keep negotiating.

Everyone would like to have things go the way they think is best. One person or group's opinion is rarely if ever completely respectful of even their own needs because they deny their need to resolve it well. And it is not respectful of the needs of the other side.

A Good Negotiation will (and should):

⇒ **Test your patience** with your own feelings and
⇒ **Test your fear** that the negotiation will fail.

If it doesn't then the outcome will not thoroughly address **the real reasons** that you have this conflict. You would just be "faking good." Faking good is a concept professionals use to understand disputants who aren't ready yet to really deal with the real issues.

Find Your Voice

In my opinion, the most important part of *your* negotiation is your work to *find your own voice*. What happens after a conflict is one's voice is destroyed for a while. And by voice I mean one's perspective on his or her circumstances in life. And this applies to conflicts that happen on any scale.

❖ The **"voice"** of a person or a people is made up of his or her own point of view, history, beliefs, values, ethics... and these come from his or her culture which usually includes family of origin, religion/philosophy of life; social and financial circumstances, and state of survival.

❖ These things make up who a person is and who *a group of people* become. When a conflict strikes deep into the heart(s) of a person or people; it profoundly changes his/her or their "voice" or perspective.

This is nature of the consequences of a conflict. Usually these changes are negative.

❖ A person's perspective or "voice" remains negative until a holistic resolution is reached to this conflict.

❖ In reaction to a conflict, a person can either experience a worsening of his or her state of life or a person can begin a process of healthy change by negotiating his/her way to a healthy resolution.

❖ To begin a process of healthy change, the first step is acknowledging that the conflict has changed your voice.
❖ Without a new voice, you will remain negative. Your actions will not only hurt others, they will hurt *you* most.

FACE The FEAR OF THE UNKNOWN

Facing the fear that you will fail to get respect and justice for your perspective is so hard that it is too difficult for most people to accept at first. It is simply human nature. During a conflict:

⇒ Our first feelings are anger, sadness, frustration...

Statements That Will Help

"Talk with someone. You need someone to just listen and care about you – not tell you that you are right, just that you have a right to feel sad, angry and frustrated."

"It doesn't mean you are right about the entire set of issues. It means you have a point and you have a right to have negative feelings. **Stop there.** It's not about getting them on your side or taking sides – it's about recognizing that you are afraid and being afraid is normal and healthy. "

*Work Through the Conflict. You **can** do it.*

"If a poisonous snake crawled in front of you – you'd be afraid right? A conflict has just as much potential to bite you and permanently harm you. The fear you have of the snake can protect you if you act on your recognition of the snake wisely."

Fear is Our Body's Way of Saying: "Stop, Think, Act Wisely."

⇒ You will be stronger if you **stop and allow yourself to feel vulnerable and relax**. Once you've experienced this feeling of weakness, the strength to face the next phase will come, and it will come more quickly and thoroughly than you ever knew possible.

Surround yourself with people who love you and spend time with them. They will help you to feel and be strong.

THE OTHER SIDE'S PERSPECTIVE

1. What if you were in the other *side/person's* situation/position? **How would you feel?**
2. Would you be afraid? Yes.
3. Would you have negative feelings about ***you*** if you switched roles?

The *other* side has their own set of negative feelings – some about you, some about the entire situation as well. They have anger, sadness, frustration, fear, and a good reason for the way they feel.

You are not simply right and "they" are wrong. The *other* side is also not "right" and you are "wrong" either.

The truth always lies somewhere in the middle.

❖ **I know this seems a fundamental truth that everyone surely understands as the basis of any argument, but what really happens to <u>prevent</u> people from negotiating is that they forget the simplicity and profound importance of this truth.**

UNDERSTANDING The FEAR:

People become blinded by their own fear that anyone will see their feelings as justified and they abandon their knowledge of the fundamental aspects of a conflict. They also fear that they will not be able to successfully negotiate a resolution that will give justice to what they need and want.

⇒ Please note that I stated respecting *your own* boundaries and needs. Often, people go too far in negotiation (when they let go of their anger). They allow and agree to points that do not respect their own vital needs.

⇒ It is important for you as a reader right here and now to understand that **I do not advocate for individuals or groups to simply give up the things that they need.** That is not a negotiation; it is a capitulation.

When you are courteous and respectful to the other side **you reveal what is *best* in you** and you open the door to an even better, more effective and efficient negotiation and resolution.

⇒ If you use your new voice and negotiate for yourself with the skills I have here - the *other side* will likely grow as well - - because they will have a better understanding of *your needs.*

⇒ Both sides will be able to let go of mistaken beliefs about the situation.

⇒ You both will have realized the reasons you may need to change.

⇒ This type of dispute resolution is called "transcendence" or transformative resolution.

Transcendence rarely happens when back room deals are struck between individuals who do not have anything to lose if the resolution isn't a good one.

Transcending Conflict is How We Grow, Heal & Prosper

All conflicts deserve the respect of transcending the situation - so that no other human is hurt in the same way again. Also, the eyes of all those around you will recognize your transcendence. They may heal and grow as well.

Transcendence is the only way we as a society grow and get better. It is the nature of what defines and creates growth from conflict. Every single conflict has the potential for transcendence if the person(s) or entities inside the conflict become strong and rise above the situation.

Ten Steps to FINDING a New Voice

1. **Write down how you feel** in a private journal, notebook, or letter to a good friend.

2. **Share this with another person** *who will <u>not</u> put you down for feeling this way.*

3. Do not say things to yourself like *"you shouldn't feel that."* **Say – It is normal or me to feel sad, pissed off...** Tell yourself: "I have a right to be angry and sad. I do not have a right to hurt someone because I feel this way."

4. **Work out these feelings** by exercising, playing sports, walking.... because I am the only person that can pour these feelings out and make them into something positive for me.

A Life Well Lived Contains Many New Chapters, Sub-Chapters & Sequels

5. **Create a new voice or version of yourself that is better.** Failures and bad times are only clay – the clay of life that I can use to mold *myself* into what I know I can be.   Without conflict, there can be no growth.

6. **Write down who you are now- because of what has happened to you.** Write down only positive things about yourself

7. **Let go** of your **negative feelings** (you can do this because you have worked through these feelings with someone else who did not make you feel bad) **You have made room for understanding** of the other sides' perspective and the entire situation.

8. **Understanding Will Lead You to Create At Least One Path** or option for resolving this that you had not been able to see before because you were blinded by the anger, frustration, fear, and pain that you didn't allow yourself to feel and work through.

9. **Generate (New) Options**. Draw yourself a table of "parking spaces" and park some new ideas. Erase the old

ones. This is called *brainstorming* ideas. It's amazing how well this imagery works to help you open up a new pathway in your heart and mind where before you had hit a wall.

What will I do now? I can do these things:

1.	2.	3.
4.	5.	6.

Refine options as you go along. Using a dry marker board works well. Erase. Use colors. Free yourself of worrying about judgments. Create new options that will work for you.

10. **Write a new statement of what I now understand and will do. You have developed your inner voice and thereby a better version of yourself.** Your new perception of this problem will make you a stronger person. Give yourself the "homework" of writing down a long version of how you feel. Here is where the development of your new voice begins.

> *"Since this happened, a lot has changed in my life.... Now I* _____ ... *and because of this I will change* _____ *And do* _____

_____
_____
_____
_____
_____
_____
_____

and negotiate this problem."

"The "Pig" (Person) That Has the Courage to STOP..."

"Doesn't run off the cliff just because everyone else is plunging to his/her own separate doom in ignorance."

"Have the courage to:"

- ❖ Stop
- ❖ Do the work, then
- ❖ Use It

"Your *Negotiation Strategy* will keep **you and the next pig from running off the cliff.**"

Chapter 3
Generating New Options:
Using The *Negotiate* Journal™

*Do not go where the path may lead,
Go instead where there is no path and leave a trail.*

Ralph Waldo Emerson

Generating New Options is the essential component of the *Negotiate* Strategy. You have a problem, obviously, because you have not been able to realize any other way to both *understand* your conflict and create options that will work for both sides. The answer is there. You can find it. The options that you will create when you complete the Negotiate Journal will form a new strategy that you will create WITH other side.

The **Negotiate Journal**™ carries you through a very simple set of questions. The answers will take some time to answer if you complete it right and to resolve something complex, you must reserve the time to think about your problem from a holistic point of view – meaning you consider the other side's perspective as well. When you do this, you unlock the closed walls, doors or barriers to succeeding and you will be free to see new options. The New **Options you will** create will come from *your* circumstances & will better address your problem.

These Options will form the foundation for Your **Strategy that you will actually create with the other side** because you will truly **Understand** your dispute holistically and this better understanding will equip you to create the best resolution. Consider the simple questions in the journal from a deep truthful perspective.

Negotiate Journal™

I. Here is What I Want To Happen:

_____
_____
_____
_____
_____

I. What I Need:

_____
_____
_____
_____
_____

II. What Does **The Other Side** Want To Happen?

_____
_____
_____
_____

II. What Does **The Other Side** Need?

_____
_____
_____
_____

Be true to how YOU would really feel if YOU were experiencing what THEY are.
Do you know exactly what they are going through? Take Time to Find Out How They Feel.

NOW compare your **want** sheets with your opponent's **want** sheets.

THEN Compare your **need** sheets with your opponent's **need** sheets.

Page 1   © Mary Kendall Hope

Negotiate Journal™

<table>
<tr><td>List Any Similar WANTS:</td><td>List Any Similar NEEDS:</td></tr>
</table>

III.   SAME WANTS   SAME NEEDS

1._____   1._____
2._____   2._____
3._____   3._____
4._____   4._____
5._____   5._____

_____
_____
_____

Now Read these lists and take some time to think.

IV.   **Create Some New Statements in your thinking based on**
            What You've Written Down.

1._____
2._____
3._____
4._____
5._____
6._____
7._____

V.   **What *Statements of Respect* Can You Use to Request**
            What You Want to Happen?

1._____
2._____
3._____

        What *Statements of Respect* Can You Use to Request
        What You Need:

1._____
2._____

Creating NEW Statements For *Yourself* – in how you now think about your problem:

This final step is an exercise in positivity - to help you create some different ways to not only *think* about this dispute but to write down new statements to tell yourself and others. Examples follow:

Example Statements for Step IV:

A. **I will do this _____ instead of that _____ specifically because it helps both of us to benefit.** Find some points to fit into these statements.

B. **This _____ is something else I will do because_____**
_____.

*Here Are Some **Statements of Respect** You Can Memorize To Help Both You & The Other Side:*

Example Statements for Step V:

C. *I will respect you because your life on this earth matters.*
   • **I would like for you to respect me by listening to me and caring about this _____ and consider doing**
   this_____
   _____.

D. ***I* will consider doing this_____ or I will consider doing that_____ because it is good for my family and it respects my/your/our needs.**

Here's a private statement (you write down for your eyes only) that will help you in settling the monetary/property portions of your issue. It prepares you when you come back to talk with the other side.

E. **I will agree to this amount _____of money paid because this _____ *specifically* will benefit me and my loved ones who could get much less than this or nothing if this negotiation goes badly.**

Here's What I Hear OFTEN as a Professional:

"The options I see or the options I have are not going to work. Or, I don't have any other options." Another response could be "I like the options *I want to use* to solve this, but the other side is not going to agree. That is why I am in conflict." **These statements are all true.**

Your *Negotiation* Journal – when you do it truthfully - will help you create a new set of options, sculpted from:

⇒ The facts,
⇒ Truths, and
⇒ Knowledge present in your conflict.

If new options do not come to light. Go LISTEN to the other side tell you their perspective <u>without</u> an interruption from *you* and think about how they feel and what they are experiencing. If that doesn't work:

Re-Do the 10 Steps to "Finding Your Voice" in Chapter 2

If you write/complete their ***Negotiate Journal*™** *before* you "find your voice" – you will likely return right back to the argument that isn't working. Working through your feelings and the entire situation and finding your voice *first* will help you to get to the place you need to be emotionally to find a holistic resolution. Then you will make the best use of your time, life energy and money.

Your conflict wasn't created in one hour; so give this process of finding your voice at least a day or two to "percolate" before you write/complete their ***Negotiate Journal*™**. A good resolution to this conflict is worth the time spent.

Think of Your Conflict as a Ball of Clay

The creation of new options can be compared to the image of a sculptor and a knotted ball of clay.

The clay represents all of your former options, ideas, facts and knowledge all combined into one entity. To this ball of clay you will add more clay from the work I am about to share with you, and from this ball of clay will come a new set of options – some of them will resemble old options, ideas and thoughts because they come from the ball of clay that is your existing conflict.

Every conflict can be placed into this paradigm or imagery. It works because all conflicts share some of the same characteristics no matter how long they have existed.

If there is dried clay, then some of it can be reconstituted with water. It depends on how long its been dried. Some of the clay from a conflict that has existed over a longer period of time cannot be reconstituted.

> ❖ **Sometimes, some things cannot be undone**. Old hurts, harms and/or injustices may not be amended. What you *can* do is focus on what *can* be molded again with water, hard work and time into something new.

The hard and prickly bumps of conflict are essentially the thorns of life that can surround a beautiful new creation when someone cares enough to craft and stimulate its growth.

Origin of This Strategy in Professional Negotiation – the BATNA

I call this your *Negotiate Strategy* because this process is not just about pulling out and re-writing options. It is also about establishing a positive strategy to truly resolve a conflict in a way that will heal as much of the past harm as possible. This is not a manipulative set of protocols.

I define **manipulative** to mean any set of skills or strategies used to further the goals of one side at the expense of the other. If you attempt to utilize these strategies with a negative intent, you will ultimately find yourself right back in your "all or nothing" thinking.

For purposes of both crediting and references my inspiration for this strategy, I include a simple definition of the professional term BATNA. The acronym defined is:

B – Best
A – Alternative
T – To a
N – Negotiated
A – Agreement
(Fisher, Ury & Patton, 1991, pp. 97-106.)

This term is still used by instructors of negotiation to teach professional negotiators. Clients come in, angry and full of their wants and needs and seek a professional for help. I use this acronym myself as an instructor of professional negotiation. As stated earlier, I like William Ury's (1981- 2011) work. He comes from Harvard Law's Program on Negotiation (PON). I believe very strongly in teaching professionally established protocols to students and professionals.

From the Public's Perspective

I created the *Negotiation* Journal™ specifically for members of the public in conflict. I believe it is a better way of thinking about this same strategy that negotiators use from *their* perspective. It also will save both you *and* the client time and energy if they write their *Negotiation* Journal *before* they begin a professional process.

❖ If you are involved in a conflict because of the complexity, career importance, or high stakes involved, *use* this process. I am providing you with an additional chapter to advise you on how to work with a good professional. A good professional can really help you change your life when you do your homework (the *Negotiate* Journal) and really take some time to consider your conflict.

Forget "Plan B" Just Keep Negotiating
You will Avoid Throwing Out the "Baby" with the Bathwater

When you are in a conflict, one of your first feelings when you consider the term "Plan B" is negative. "Plan B" is second rate and not as good. Stop. Stop thinking of options as either "good" or "bad" because life is not that easy. Instead of thinking of one's alternatives as "plan B" or "plan C" just stop using that terminology all together when it comes to facing a conflict. Focus your energy on resolving it right. It may take several tries, but if you keep with the right strategy, then the resulting resolution will produce healing and transformation. If you throw out the "baby" with the bathwater, you'll lose parts of Plan A that were important.

❖ **One of the best strengths anyone *has* is the ability to empower him or herself with an open mind.**

So Empower Yourself, REVISE the options that are not working and create in your minds as an image of clay. Let the images sit for a while on the potter's wheel while you imagine preparing a new sculpture.

A new creation comes from a new image in *your* mind. You create this image by eliminating the bad ways you think about this conflict. Remember, the "bad" things you have been thinking, saying, and doing have not worked.

❖ You must accept that you are **not** going to get all of what you **want.**

❖ If you begin with that expectation you will succeed in getting what you **need** and you may get **more needs met for not only yourself but those around you** who can either benefit from your skill at negotiating your problem or feel the awful consequences when you do not get your needs met.

Remember the professional term, BATNA (Fisher, Ury & Patton, 1991). The reason it was conceived was to assist individuals to understand that the N & A (negotiated agreement) would never include 100% of what a client came in wanting. The reason it's still used to teach negotiators today is after three decades, it is still true.

Develop Some New Beliefs

1. **Recognize** what you are going through and
2. **Stop.**
3. **Have a meeting** with *yourself,*
4. **Find your voice**, and
5. **Write your "Negotiation Strategy."**

The best thing to begin the negotiation with (when you meet with the client or the other side) is your *Negotiation* Journal memorized a fresh set of blank paper.

*You can do it. Write Your Best **Negotiation Journal**™*

Keep the rest of your notes in a briefcase or zippered case until they are needed. Assure that you do not just whip out your needs and say, "let's go down this list."

❖ Think of your work to write your *Negotiation* Journal as

the work that a coach does with his team before hitting the field. They do not usually bring their notes; they simply come together and play. You will simply come together and **negotiate.**

If you both want to resolve this (and you need to assume that they do) – **you both together will create a new more specific set of options.** *Do not for one moment think that the other side does not have a very big need to resolve this well. They do.*

What *you* think the other person has written as their *wants* and *needs* will be different from what they would write.

- Whether big or small, the differences aren't as bad as you think.
- The small differences **are not only *why* you are in conflict in the first place.**

These are Some of the Best Kept Secrets to Negotiating A Holistic Resolution.

Someone wise once told me that there are only a couple of steps between "first class" and "coach" on an airplane, but these are an important couple of steps.

- ⇒ **To both you and the other "side" these small nuances mean everything.**
- ⇒ Respect each and every aspect of these nuances and show that respect when you are working with the other side.
- ⇒ No matter what you may have felt about them in the past, let it go.

In negotiation, mediation, or facilitation:

The small nuances are the things that are the most difficult to talk about. Sometimes, these things are ugly or taboo. **Sometimes, there haven't been ways to talk about these things before in this person's life**, *so they did not know how to talk to you about them.*

One of the things I teach new professional <u>mediators</u> is: "Do not go into this field if you are not strong enough to handle the ugly side of life." (Hope, 2009; 2014a).

People have conflicts because they do not know how to work through the "ugly" aspects of daily living.

As a professional, you become a buffer for negative thoughts and feelings, but also you will be able to empower your clients to really commit to working through the hard parts of writing their *Negotiate* Journal™ and Re-Writing it - as the agreement or action plan with the other side.

After healing begins, growth and transcendence follows in time. Everyone around you (your clients certainly, and other professionals) will benefit from your hard work to write the best *Negotiation Strategy* possible for every negotiation.

Chapter 4

Prepare To Negotiate Successfully

An eye for an eye only ends up making the whole world blind.

Mahatma Gandhi

Respect is Just as Contagious as Violence

If you have taken the time to write out how you feel and how you think the other person feels about this dispute, you are probably wondering: What options would the other side have written down if they wrote their own *Negotiate Journal*™? Where would the similarities happen between both sets of options? You'll soon find out.

If you have had the courage to be honest with yourself, you've completed an *Negotiate Journal*™ that truly caused you to pause. You've taken some time to think, hopefully you've taken one or two nights to sleep on it. If you've really considered this from the other side's perspective, then you've realized that you've worked hard and succeeded in rising above the situation.

Do not expect the other side to be positive and open-minded

Expect to see them having negative feelings and making negative statements. That way, when it happens, it won't crush your new positive attitude. Just expect the other side to behave badly because they might. Do not try and change their negative feelings. Just allow them to have these feelings. Allow them to say what they need to say.

What's your role?

Listen.

Respond with respect. Do not engage in an argument, even if you feel what they are saying is wrong. Maybe they are making ugly statements about you. Maybe they are stating untruths. Let them.

⇒ The other side may still be in a negative place because they are experiencing pain. Pain is a lot like heat from a burning furnace. It boils up and releases out like hot steam – often without stimulation or reason. **Step back in time, space, and response**. I teach this to children.

⇒ **If someone is yelling at you – step back**. Create some space between you and them first.

⇒ **Allow some time to go by before you respond**. And respond **slowly,** with <u>few </u>words and

⇒ **Choose words that are positive and show respect to *you* and the other side**.

These actions alone will do two needed things much more powerfully than if you yell back or make negative statements back.

1. It will immediately **set a healthy boundary of imagery and words**. This boundary will begin a new set of expectations in the other. They will immediately recognize that it is not all right for them to talk to you in this way.

2. It will **create a new standard for interaction between you and the other side**. There will be a new tone in the room, and if you keep yourself together and stick to your positivity, limited words, and respect – it

will immediately convey to the other side that this interaction is going to be different. It is going to be respectful and positive.

Take a moment to drink a sip of water and either say nothing or apologize and say one or two words of respect. Take another moment if you need to find some respectful words. These words of respect will change the entire situation. Respect is just as contagious as violence.

Remember, you may falter at any point in this new discussion and get mad. If the other side takes a moment to forgive you – how grateful you will be that they did. Do not expect them to do this, but it is good to take note of it when it happens, and maybe state appreciation when appropriate.

❖ **Do** recognize and appreciate *their* respect if and when they do begin to talk positively to *you*. If you do, I believe you'll soon see the same respect given to you in turn.

NEGOTIATE _
Assure you both have plenty of time to talk without demands on your schedule. Turn off phones, televisions and any other distraction. Assure the area you talk is comfortable with a nice restroom close by that is clean and pleasant. (It is very helpful during breaks to go to a restroom that is clean and smells nice.) Remember, every break is likely to involve a restroom stop.

Talking about a conflict is one of the most stressful things you can do. Give yourself every advantage to succeed. It may sound simple to create a nice restroom in advance (close to where you plan to talk to this person), but it's important. I've been there with thousands of individuals in conflict, and sometimes, your trip to the restroom is a crucial moment of privacy to breathe, think, and re-group. Make this atmosphere as pleasant as you can. New professionals smirk when I teach them this; experienced professionals nod their heads.

Here are some detailed *Negotiation* Statements that form the *Negotiate Strategy* ™

I recommend using these in the 1ˢᵗ Meeting

1. "Thank you for making time to talk."

2. "I brought some paper and pens for both of us in case we want to write down what we agree on."

*Use the word **agree** as often as it applies, you want to promote a new way of thinking about this dispute.*

3. "First I want to take time to listen to what/ how you want to work this out."

4. LISTEN to what they have to say without interrupting them. Take time to THINK about what they have said so you can

5. **SUMMARIZE** briefly what you've heard without disagreeing with anything.
   "I just want to make sure I understood what you said."

Then USE THEIR EXACT WORDS.

Do not take this opportunity to correct them or interject your own description from *your* perspective, just repeat back what you heard.

6. "Thank you for telling me that." "Now that I've listened to you without interruption, would you do the same for me?"

7. "I want to share my experience of this with you. It may sound different than your experience, but this is how I feel about it."

8. TELL YOUR SIDE RESPECTFULLY and BRIEFLY WITHOUT ARGUING
   "I want to briefly tell you what I *want* to happen and what I *need* to happen."

9. "Then I want you to tell me what *you* want to happen and what you *need* to happen."

10. "I would like to write these things down. Do you mind if we make some notes. I believe it will help us work this out."

SLOWLY WORK THROUGH Your Stories, Wants, Needs, and Find your Common Ground.

Do not expect this to take 30 minutes or even one hour. Expect it to take several days or longer, depending on the depth of this dispute and the long-term consequences of this dispute. If your dispute was created over years of time, it will not just *work out* immediately. You may make one of these statements above then take an hour or more before you are ready to go to the next step.

❖ The other side will eventually begin to talk positively to you. It may come in starts and stops, but it will come.
❖ Recognize when it does and say **"Thank you for that."** When you thank people for hard work, they are likely to do something again for you.

The key here is recognizing respect.

When your clients are caught up in a conflict, it is easy to overlook and not recognize when the other side is either respecting them and/or agreeing with them. It is your job as a professional negotiator to recognize when points are agreed on and highlight these moments. When you do, you help them to lay the groundwork for a more sustainable resolution.

❖ Write down points that you and the other side agree on and recognize (out loud) when the other side is respecting *you*. This one of the keys to success because it is genuinely what is needed to stimulate both your client and the other side to work through this conflict and resolve it.

The other side of a conflict (who has **_not_** done their own *Negotiation* Journal or who did *not* work on it as hard as your client did) may need more time to truly show them the respect they need.

Delayed Respect in the Other Side

This is such an important concept to understand and utilize positively to help you that I'm doing to give you a few more secrets about what you will face when you come to the table with the opposing side.

If you slip and get angry, stop yourself.

❖ Sometimes, the other side *wants* to show you respect. They come to a table to talk to you and they *intended* to talk respectfully to you – but then they open their mouths and ugliness comes out. Or, they begin to talk and get off topic onto other hurtful things or other unresolved conflicts.

Expect this. It is the nature of dealing with conflict. Talking about conflict brings up a garbage bag or laundry bag (both images are directly applicable) of unresolved conflicts because all of a sudden, the topic is "conflicts" so people bring everything and the kitchen sink up. Expect this. Listen respectfully without interruption for a few minutes. Then respectfully interrupt them with the statement:

"I hear you and I am understanding what you are saying. I want us to agree to "table" this for now because it needs the respect of us dealing with it. Let me just ask you *this* about the *first thing* we agreed to talk about today...."

You have respectfully changed the subject, refocusing it back onto the original objective. It is the right thing to do. If you allow the discussion to be side-tracked into every tangential aspect of your problem at hand, you will not be able to build the success you need to forge an agreement.

❖ If you forge an agreement on something *solvable* today, then you are better equipped down the road to come back to the table and talk about another issue.

Trust me. It is the discipline you will need to come to an agreement that builds a new relationship and a new way of interacting.

This is what you need right now the most – to build a new atmosphere of respect.

You can go back quickly into your old way of interacting if you do not stay focused and reinforce your common interests, strengths, and points agreed on.

Respect sometimes success comes in starts and stops. In fact, *your* respect of the other side may also be displayed or *perceived* by the other side as coming in "starts and stops" as well.

❖ They may <u>not be</u> able to perceive your actions as respectful for a while, because they are blinded by their beliefs and negative feelings.

You will likely get respect back in a shorter frame of time if you keep showing the other side respect.

Respect IS just as contagious as violence under the right circumstances. It just doesn't get the sensational "press" coverage.

BRING IT ON

Come to the table with humility, self-respect (of your own needs) and a **fresh set of blank paper.** Some of this is a review from chapter three but important to reiterate. Do not bring your filled in sheets from your *Negotiate Journal*™ and say "This is the way I am looking at this – don't you think what I've written is right?" It is tempting, because if you have worked on an effective *Negotiation Strategy* that went deep into the issues and honestly addressed them - you've both invested a lot of hard work. That hard work was not wasted, it is more valuable to you than gold.

Just know this, and come to the table to talk and bring your most positive self.

> ❖ **Bring pencils, erasers, calculator and colored highlighters along with flip charts, pens, extra legal pads, healthy snacks and beverages…** so you can work together on creating this agreement. Empower yourself with the right tools for your objective.

Your goal here is to help yourself to succeed and simultaneously, you will be helping the other side to feel less stressed and empowered. Bring everything that you think will make it easy. Stop at a reasonable hour for dinner and for the evening. Individuals in conflict need more time for breaks, rest, snacks, meals, and just to consider the dramatic changes that they are working on (from their life perspective) than you may anticipate.

Take a break when things are going well.

Think about how much you have accomplished on that break instead of thinking about anything that is negative. If negative thoughts start coming up, then go find one of your trusted supportive friends (*that is neutral and has no stake in this conflict*) and go have dinner with them. Focus on everything *positive* about what has transpired. This will help you when you are not sure about these new options you are considering. You need to give validity to the hard work done in negotiating your position.

> ❖ If you have negative thoughts or feelings, jot these thoughts down *privately* for your eyes only to read. Do not bring these negative statements back into the next discussion. This will tear down your good foundation for success that you have worked so hard to create.

Think of a sports team coming back from a time out and allowing negativity to steal their power and confidence. The team would lose their momentum and likely lose the game. So stay focused on what you've built. It is easy to fall back into the old patterns that tore you apart and caused you to fail before. Remember what you have to lose and what you have to gain by succeeding.

WORKING OUT AN AGREEMENT

Start a separate sheet of paper because if you are continuing to respect one another and communicate positively, you are likely beginning to create an agreement.

1. Write Statements Down That Both Agree On

2. **Do not throw away any of the sheets of paper that you have jointly worked on.** There are likely golden nuggets of truth on these that just need re-writing and refining in a finalized agreement.

3. Use EXACT Phrases, Words, concepts that strike you as true and Positive.

4. Re-write/Refine it until the agreement respects both sides equally

5. SEE the Next Page

Patience During the Last Half & End

Expect the *writing* of your agreement to take just as long as it took you to come to an agreement.

This way you will not be frustrated when it does take time.

In my experience, the best agreemen are those that take lot of time to writ

Take Your Time, Work it Out

You also want to place several nights of sleep between you and a final agreement so you can digest the changes that are occurring in your life and are about to occur when you begin to implement this agreement. Yes. **This process is about real *change* and doing it**

right. In my experience, **to do anything else is a waste of precious lifetime,** feelings, and money.

As your agreement takes form and becomes more and more specified to what you both need, then continue feel free to start a new sheet of paper and re-write it *again*.

Do Not Re-Think Things You Agree On. Stick To What You Agree On. Just refine it.

Work to write an agreement that both of you feel good about. Refine the points you agree on with much patience – the small details are important. Change any small detail that doesn't "wreck" the entire agreement.

Make changes that will strengthen the agreement not weaken it. Remember your common interests when you are tempted to change the big points you agree on.

5. Set a date to **call the other side back and check on how it's going in about two months** after you have written the agreement. Set it sooner if needed, but don't go past three months without checking in.

Do not skip this step. If this process has gone well, no matter what the prior circumstances, call the other side and "check in" and amend anything needed.

The fact that you may need to amend the agreement due to changes in work schedules or just life in general is a good, healthy and needed thing to do. Expect to amend it slightly. This call back will help the other side to know that you care, and caring is what will help you both to not only transform this conflict into a "change" life brought – the caring will also help you transcend it.

When you transcend the conflicts that life brings you – you empower yourself to become better at everything else in your life.

Chapter 5

Types of PROFESSIONALPRACTICE

*The best way to destroy an enem
is to make him a frien*

Abraham Lincoln

Negotiation: The Foundation of Dispute Resolution

The general public often confuses the terms negotiation; mediation; arbitration; and facilitation as the same, and they are *not* the same. All use the skills of negotiation but mediation, facilitation, arbitration, and counseling employ neutral professionals to use specific sets of skills to help resolve the conflict.

This simple chapter is vital to the public because:

In the business of our every day lives, most people have not yet placed the above professions (**mediation, facilitation, negotiation**...) into their "go to" *response* to a presented conflict... until now.

Negotiation is when a hired professional advocates or talks in support of one side's perspective. It is also when an attorney is hired to represent one person's perspective or a group's perspective. That person/group could have a conflict in a:

❖ Personal Dispute with another individual
❖ Work Setting as an Employee

- ❖ Business Setting as a client, the employer, or between businesses or organizations
- ❖ In a Community Setting such as a club, church, or other organized community group or in a
- ❖ Political Governing Body on a local, national or international level.

Negotiation can involve more than one of these categories simultaneously. Either one or both sides may have hired attorneys, representatives, or paid professionals to negotiate their position.

Just to reiterate, a simple negotiation does *not* have a third party that is neutral assisting *both* sides to come to a resolution. However, it is always in the best interests of a professional or attorney to reach a resolution that holistically addresses both the financial and emotional aspects of the dispute because conflicts are seldom if ever created over money and property alone.

⇒ The feelings of those involved (which include their principles of ethics) are always the reason that humans reach the point of *needing* outside help to attain a resolution.

Mediation utilizes a trained third party professional to help two opposing sides to reach a resolution to a conflict. Both sides negotiate for their own position, but a mediator is neutral and assists the opposing sides to communicate with one another in a way that balances the power of the discussion.

- Balancing the power assures that both sides are given equal respect, equal strength of their position, and equal time to speak.
- The goal of mediation is to write an agreement that will specifically address the *objectives* that are brought to a mediator.

Mediation is utilized in nearly every area of conflict from divorces, to international conflicts, business conflicts, property disputes, personal disputes and family challenges such as estate planning mediation.

It is an extremely effective professional practice when used by a trained and credentialed professional to resolve two party and multi-party conflicts. Mediation offerings differ in each state within the U.S., but the following sub-types are often available

Types of Mediation in Current Practice (most states)

- Domestic Disputes (Neighbors or Personal)
- Property Settlement (Divorce)
- Child Custody (Divorce)
- Landlord Tenant
- Estate Planning
- Workman's Compensation
- Personal Injury
- Work place employer/employee EOE
- Business to Business Financial Settlement
- Organization to Business Disputes
- International Mediation is Used World-Wide to settle business and political conflicts.

Legal Representation/ Attorney

An **Attorney** is a hired professional legal representative of you or the group you represent. Attorneys are negotiators who will meet with you, ask you want you want to happen and work through the legal process in the state or country in which you live. Attorneys usually work with you to write a set of goals targeted toward legal intervention. This is why I recommend to you to find your voice and write/complete an *Negotiate Journal™. before* you go and meet with an attorney,

Attorneys are *not* trained to process emotional stories. They are trained to focus on facts and to concentrate on the legal aspects that pertain to your case. If you sort out your conflict before you go to see an attorney, then you will have the *best* chance of focusing your time and energy on the legality of the dispute.

Your Attorney Works for *YOU*

Attorneys serve a vital role in our society to negotiate and win disputes, but they are there for a purpose – to use their knowledge of the law to negotiate your case. It is easy to allow an attorney to simply take over for you. This means they will negotiate the best they know how for you. They will use what they know and their skill (**which will be absent of *your* specific feelings**) to obtain a settlement.

Attorneys are trained to remove emotion from the conflict. Sometimes, this is best. Sometimes, it is not. Your emotions are what make you human. First, give justice to what you feel. The best way for your perspective to be resolved is for you to use your *own voice* to negotiate your perspective and utilize your attorney's skill and knowledge of the law to assure your voice is heard.

So develop your voice *before* you let them speak for you.

- ❖ **Present a clear list of what you want to negotiate to your attorney.** Do not just say – "I want you to work this out for me." If you do that, the attorney will work off his/her own agenda. Be certain of your new perspective. This way when the attorney asks you questions, you'll have clear directives. Do not default to "You just solve it," or allow for confusion this will just convolute the problem. Be certain of what you need and will offer as options.

- ❖ **Keep yourself *inside* the negotiation**, rather than allowing your attorney to conduct closed-door meetings without you. If you can control yourself, then be the person that negotiates all points of your agreement.

- ❖ If you cannot control yourself, then **step back** and realize this. Listen to those around you who encourage you to control your anger. Take a break from meetings so you do not cost yourself unnecessary legal fees.

Counseling is one of the least expensive and best options available to individuals in conflict. It is a private choice and I recommend that you keep it your private business. The general public does not know how to respond well to the news that you are going to counseling – and in not knowing how to respond, people often misjudge, mislabel and generally say the wrong things in response to news that you are seeking a professional counselor to help you. So, do not make this public knowledge.

- ❖ Licensed Counselors can help you sit down with someone and work something out confidentially *outside* of a mediation setting or any other professional dispute resolution. Counselors are trained in how to respond to you and keep your discussion healthy and positive. They are also trained to just talk to you in private. Both state and federal laws mandate licensed counselors to maintain confidentiality.

"Do not feel like something is wrong with you if a mediator, negotiator, arbitrator or facilitator privately recommends counseling time to you to resolve something. The professional is *not* making a negative judgment; they are trying to help you. Working out an in-depth problem that arises during the resolution of a conflict in counseling happens all the time. It will save you money to work it out with a counselor and will truly help you best in the long run."

Arbitration is the use of a credentialed professional to decide the outcome of a conflict. An arbitrator in essence acts as a judge. His or Her decision can be either **binding** - meaning that it cannot be brought again to a court of law in the exact same manner – or nonbinding. **Nonbinding** means that the case can be brought in the exact same manner to a regular court of law to overturn the non-binding decision. Both binding and nonbinding decisions (if not disputed in a regular court of law) may stand as the final resolution to the conflict.

❖ In most states, it is not usually a public choice to arbitrate a dispute. It is more often a mandated option in a contract.

If attorneys *choose* to arbitrate a case it is usually to "rehearse" how they would present such a case in a lawsuit - if they don't like the arbitrator's judgment. If they *like* the judgment that is given by the arbitrator, you (their client) have saved money by avoiding a lawsuit.

An arbitrator acts alone to decide what resolution is best - based on what is presented to him or her by both sides. Both sides may have attorneys to represent them in arbitration or only one side may have an attorney.

Arbitration is usually mandated in business contracts as the only method of resolution of a dispute. Some credit cards and other business agreements between a company and customer have arbitration as the method of resolution if there is a dispute between the customer and business (specified in the contract). Some contracts between sports talent and sports organizations that hire talent *specify* arbitration as the method for dispute resolution. Businesses do this to avoid costly court lawsuits. Read your contacts that you sign carefully.

Members of the *public* do not usually choose to have a case arbitrated. One must check the availability of arbitrators in the state you live in and in the state in which the dispute originated. You would also need to check to assure that arbitration would be the best option for resolving your dispute. Check your state's court system statutes to see if the option of arbitrating your conflict will be upheld in a court of law if it has not been mandated by contract.

Facilitation is the use of a trained conflict resolution professional to assist a group of individuals to resolve an issue or set of issues.

Facilitators help groups such as:
- City councils,
- School boards,
- Governing bodies for state or national entities,
- Small or large businesses,
- Business departments/divisions or
- Public or private organizations

To resolve:
1. Public Relation issues,
2. Wide-spread challenges,
3. Major changes or
4. Internal disputes.

A facilitator may also assist any group to solve a large single problem or a collective set of problems that it faces.

EXAMPLE 1 - A college may employee a facilitator to work with its governing board to address a widespread campus issue that requires fundamental changes to the college's charter or mission. Let's say an "all male" college faces the challenge of repeated female applicants and this issue gets national press coverage...

⇒ A facilitator could help the college to address the question of changing the college to allow female students and change the college to "co-ed" status. Such a change has happened often in history and it impacts nearly every aspect of a college and its surrounding community and financial support structure.

EXAMPLE 2 - A business might hire a facilitator to help them develop a new division within an existing department. Changes within an organization can create deep internal conflicts when employees fear losing their jobs or major changes to existing methods of doing things.

EXAMPLE 3 - School boards often hire facilitators to help them to make school closing changes and adjustments and seek the best ways to deliver this news to the communities that these changes affect.

⇒ As businesses change, so do the choices of what they need to provide. Making these choices is very difficult without outside *objective* help that is trained to help a group to examine options and discuss the positive points and negative downsides to existing policy.

The skills a facilitator can bring to an organization or business can assist a group to face a financial or personnel challenge *well* instead of poorly. Facilitators use a specific set of skills *designed* to assist groups in these complex problems.

Victims Advocate

A **victim's advocate** is a trained professional who researches an individual's case and speaks in support of a specific individual (victim) in a court of law. A victim's advocate can also speak for and support the voice of a victim in meetings with police officials, criminals, or other professionals as needed. They do not speak for the offender.

Victims are individuals who have been identified as having experienced abuse or criminal violence to the point that their emotional ability to speak for themselves has been weakened to the point that they need support to meet their own survival needs. They may sign written permission for their V.A. to work along side their counselor to help them together when needed.

A child advocate may speak on behalf of children in a court setting when their parents are either unable to speak for them or have been accused of abuse or neglect.

Chapter 6

Use Your *Negotiate* Journal™
With a Professional

Change is the law of life.
And those who look only to the past
or present
are certain to miss the future.

John F. Kennedy

You know your situation best. If your friends think you should just get a counselor or a lawyer they may be correct, but consider what I am recommending to you because you have to be your own best counselor to yourself. *The statements I include in this chapter are general statement recommendations. Of course you will respond/recommend based on the specifics of each case with professional protocols in mind.*

Go to see a professional. Do not worry about what other people will think or worry about explaining why you are seeking out a mediator or other professional. It's your private business. Just tell others that you are working on it. They don't need to know anything else.

Tell others positive things *only*. This will keep *you* positive.

Remember, you do not have to tell the general public about the negative aspects of *anything*. Often, members of the general public thrive off the conflicts of others, so it is best not to give the general public anything to gossip about. Keep yourself strong so you can really work on this in private.

It's likely that your problem can be served by several of these professional categories. Here's a guide to help you. If **Children** Are Involved or the Conflict is **Between You & A Spouse**:

Counseling is your best option first. You need the respect of time that counseling gives you to resolve the interpersonal issues.

Mediators, Negotiators, Facilitators, Arbitrators, and Attorneys do not have the background or professional objective to assist you to address interpersonal issues that you may need to address. Also, professionals in these fields typically charge much more per hour for their time.

It is best to not waste money on legal fees when you need to spend some time working through interpersonal issues.

❖ **You can bring your *Negotiate Journal*™ right into a counseling session.** A counselor's objective is to help you and this worksheet would provide a good road map for working through the intangible aspects of your dispute.

❖ Counseling is an excellent option. It is confidential and as I stated in the previous chapter, it is best to *not* reveal to others that you seek counseling simply because it is your own private business.

As a licensed counselor of many years I can tell you from experience that it is the wisest of individuals who choose to go to counseling and truly work through their interpersonal challenges first. I have been blessed in my career with the opportunity to stand with many an individual, youth, couple and family after they have done some very hard work and found a peace that wouldn't have happened without it.

Mediation

If your dispute is attached or may potentially be attached to a court issue (and most dispute have this potential) then agreeing to mediate the case first is an excellent option.

- ❖ If you successfully mediate the case *out* of court you will save yourself money, time, and you will have an opportunity to resolve the deeper aspects of the dispute.

Bring The Final Edit of your *Negotiate Journal*™ to Mediation *or* your best list of needs, wants, and common interests. This will greatly help you to maximize your time in mediation. It will help you tell your story more succinctly and thoroughly. A well-mediated case usually avoids lawsuit.

If you can avoid a lawsuit, do so. If you mediate the dispute, you will also have an opportunity to create an environment for healing and positive foundation for a new future if you work toward this and truly commit to what it takes to make this happen.

Negotiation

If your dispute is between you and a business or other professional entity, seeking a professional negotiator will help. Also, if the other side in your dispute has a negotiator or attorney representing them, you need one as well to balance the power.

When one side has either an attorney or professional negotiator and the other side doesn't the power of the side (that doesn't have a professional) is automatically diminished and the outcome has a high possibility of not going in the favor of the person without an attorney or negotiator to assist him or her.

Also, negotiators are very beneficial and commonly used between certain types of business disputes. These include:

- Union/large business owner disputes;
- Business/business disputes
- Large business salary establishment/contracts;

- Police Negotiators (specially trained) for crime, hostage, and barricade situations
- National organizational disputes (NAACP; Political Groups);
- National/international diplomatic and political conflicts

Working Diligently with a Professional

Bring A Good Draft of your *Negotiate* Journal to Negotiation

Your list of needs, wants, and common interests need not be perfect because as the negotiator you will know exactly what your client is working on and can immediately help him/her finish it. Bringing the best draft will greatly help your client to maximize his/her time in negotiation, because he/she will have started what a good negotiation process needs to succeed.

Attorneys/Legal Representation If you are involved in a dispute in which very large sums of money or property are at stake, you will need to retain an attorney(s) to not only represent you and your position, but also advise you on legal statutes that apply to your case and research the best legal precedents that may apply to your case.

Having an attorney working for you is wise in a dispute in which the outcome will definitely change your life circumstances. If you are about **to lose** either:

- Your job,
- Home,
- Freedom,
- Survival from loss of money or
- The other side in your dispute has an attorney…

Then you should obtain legal representation. You can use every single aspect of this book, and other professional assistance (such as counseling, mediation, negotiation or arbitration) as well, but you should get an attorney if your dispute meets the above criteria. Get informed about how you can obtain legal assistance if you have limited funds.

Bring Polished List of Options from your *Negotiate Journal*™ to

Your First Meeting with An Attorney

Attorneys stay focused on the legal aspects of your dispute. When you have the best draft ready of what you want, need, and common interests you believe exist, then share these with your attorney.

❖ If your dispute is not serious but the other side <u>has</u> an attorney, then attempt to talk to the other side *without* their attorney (unless you are legally prohibited from doing so).

HERE'S SOME FREE ADVICE I GIVE TO CLIENTS AS A LICENSED COUNSELOR

If you sense that the other side may use every single word you say against you, then do not attempt to talk to them. If the other side will not negotiate in good faith, then resolution may have to come from a court decision.

Facilitation

If you own or are in the management structure of a business or organization that is experiencing a dispute or conflict that the governing board has attempted to resolve on three or more occasions unsuccessfully, then a facilitator may really help you. The most important things a facilitator helps an organization or group save is:

1. Money
2. Public perception
3. Time
4. Valuable energy/resources

A good facilitator will come into an organization that has problems and immediately help the situation because a facilitator brings direction, discipline, organization, understanding and a step-by-step process for dealing with the problem.

Choose facilitation:

- If you are in a business that is losing large sums of *money* or *employees* and have been doing so for a very long time.

- If your church or religious organization keeps losing one pastor or church leader after another (and you are in a position to suggest professional help)

- If you are a part of a large organization that is facing a tremendous set of changes, a scandal,

Working It Out
  With a Small Group

A good facilitator could help all of these problems.

Bring A Good Draft of your *Negotiate Journal* to Facilitation

"Your list of needs, wants, and common interests do not need to be perfect because the facilitator will understand what you are working on and can integrate your work into the facilitation process.

As with other professions listed here, it will greatly help you to maximize your time in *facilitation*, to work on a *Negotiation Strategy*. You will have started a portion what the facilitator would have worked with you to *refine* in the middle to latter part of the facilitation process.

Facilitation utilizes a slightly different set of steps to generate an action plan, but the work you complete will help you to formulate your problem and more efficiently generate options, establish criteria and eventually write an action plan.

Arbitration

Arbitration is generally not a profession that you call to request service from as a member of the general public unless arbitrators are available in your state to hear disputes or your attorney recommends this.

Sometimes, individuals and their attorneys choose to arbitrate a case to see how the case might play out in court. You would seek advisement from your attorney on this. Presenting a case to an arbitrator is much like presenting it to a judge, because an arbitrator acts as a judge in the case. The arbitrator hears both sides then he/she decides who and what specifically will be done.

♦ If you are involved in a dispute with a business or organization and you have signed a contract with this entity, read your contract.

Many businesses state how a dispute between you and that business will be resolved. Some do not specify this – in which case you would use your own good negotiation skills to resolve the dispute. Other contracts specify mediation and even negotiation. Many contracts specify that disputes will be settled with arbitration. (See my definition previous chapter). If this is the case, then if you wish to engage in resolution of this dispute with this business or organization then you must go through the arbitration process.

♦ Prepare your case as if you are an attorney with all notes, facts, and documents that you need and bring these to the arbitration.

Bring A Polished List from your *Negotiate Journal*™ to Arbitration

Your list of needs, wants, and common interests may be read out to the arbitrator if he/she requests this. You may want to specifically request to read your options/needs yourself – if your attorney advises this.

Present your side to the arbitrator. The arbitrator will ask questions. The other side will present their case. The arbitrator will then decide the outcome of the case.

If you decide or must arbitrate a dispute, the case you present to the arbitrator must be as specific as possible. If the case has significant consequences to you, then I recommend seeking an attorney to assist you.

Victim's Advocacy

If you have been the victim of domestic violence, criminal assault or any other criminal offense or abuse then a victim's advocate will be of great assistance to you.

♦ This professional will go with you to court or may assist you with police matters utilizing police protocol. They will be able to help individuals to find safe housing if this is needed and will be able to confidentially assist with obtaining counseling and any other services you may need.

Advocates assist children who do not have appropriate parental help and they may assist anyone who is in a position of challenge to their survival because of a dispute or history of disputes or alleged crime or violence.

Bring A Polished List from your *Negotiate Journal*™ to Victim's Advocacy Meeting in Court or in an Organized Meeting

Your list of needs, wants, and common interests may be read out to the offender when this is called for in court or the pre-arranged meeting.

Before your formal meeting with the offender, you can bring your best draft of your *Negotiate Journal*™ to your advocate and work with the advocate to refine your needs, wants and common interests.

It is important to note that anyone involved in a dispute with an alleged abuser may not be suitable for mediation. Mediation requires an equal power balance and if an individual is significantly weaker due to past emotional trauma that presently affects the dispute they may be in, a power imbalance will be present.

64

Individuals who will benefit from victim's advocacy will usually also benefit from simultaneous legal representation.

*   *   *

STEPS For USING This STRATEGY with A PROFESSIONAL

NEGOTIATION with Legal Representation:

1. **First, write/complete your *Negotiate Journal*™** then contact the "other" side and schedule a time to talk to them. Work out as much of the dispute as you can if the other side genuinely wants to work this out – it will help you both.

2. Select either an attorney or professional negotiator

3. **Bring your *Negotiate Journal*™** that you have re-written/edited **to** **your** **meeting** with the attorney/negotiator.

4. **Schedule a time** with the other side **to negotiate** with both attorneys present or without attorneys present. If one side does not have an attorney, then wait until one can be found through legal-aid and both of you have equal numbers of professionals a the negotiation table. **We are not talking about time spent in front of a judge. In lawsuits, individuals have different numbers of attorneys. Negotiation is a step to avoid a lawsuit and /or trial by jury.

5. **Expect** that the negotiation process is going **to take longer than you think** to resolve

6. Expect that the **writing of the** actual contract or agreement you are negotiating will **take a long time instead of happening quickly**. A well-written contract that lasts and really resolves an issue is one that is amended repeatedly during the writing process.

7. If this process goes really quickly, then stop and consider how it is going between each step. Ask yourself if you are

really resolving the conflict? If you are, **keep going and see it through to completion.**

8. If you do not think you are, then contact your negotiator/attorney and let them know the specifics of what is *not* being addressed. You both may be either **"faking good" or "saving face"**. These are two coping skills professionals see in nearly every conflict. These are not actions deliberately undertaken to manipulate the situation, **they are just reactions that people instinctively display** when they do not have the knowledge, confidence or support to really deal with what they have been presented. **Stop. Use your 10-Steps to Find Your Voice** and Re-Write Your *Negotiate Journal*™ and you will find some deeper truth that will help you *really* resolve it.

9. Consider taking some time to **respectfully talk to the other side**. If you do this right the first time you will save much stress, time, money, and feelings in the future.

10. When you talk to the other side, bring blank pages to the table and **create solutions together** and deal with issues with the other side **exactly as chapters 3-4 suggests**. Work through any issues you think aren't being addressed. Do not feel pressured to just sign something. It is more common that folks need to make adjustments in agreements to assure that they have done it right.

For a MEDIATION:

1. First, **write/complete your** *Negotiate Journal*™ then contact the "other" side and schedule a time to talk to them. Work out as much of the dispute as you can.

2. Sometimes, the court will assign you a mediator or you may be able to hire your own. If you hire a professional, then **select someone you feel you trust and has sound skill to help you**. You need to have faith in your mediator and feel good about the guidance you receive to resolve your dispute.

3. Contact the mediator and schedule a time to meet him or her in person to assess that you trust this person and feel that they are skilled enough to help you to solve your issue.

Talk briefly to the mediator about how they will run the mediation – what will happen first, second, third, then next and last...

Talk Honestly With The Professional

You have a right to know this. If you do not like or connect with the mediator, hire someone else. Many are out there and all have different backgrounds of experience, training, and credentials.

Do not talk to them about the specifics of your dispute before mediation.
This would *bias* the mediator and you need the mediator to remain neutral. Neutrality is what makes mediation such a good

4. Mediators will send you **"Agreement to Mediate"** documents for you to read and sign. Ask them to simply explain this contract in person and every document you will either sign or write. Mediators are there to help you. Allow them to help you. Assure you understand what is going to happen in your case if you reach agreement or if you don't. Assure you understand what will happen in your next court/date or hearing because the agreements reached or not reached will change the court process and next hearing date.

5. Bring blank paper to the mediation. Refer to your *Negotiate Journal*™ notes in private to help you present your side. But **never present "demands" just trust the process** and make respectful requests to the other side.

6. Most agreements require that points agreed on are specific with dates and time written into the agreement. So take paper, pencils, highlighters and a calculator to the mediation meetings so you are prepared. Your mediator will have these, but **you may want to use a calculator**

yourself on a break for lunch to help you think in private.

7. Relax. The mediator is there to help you. **Allow the process to work.** If you've done your *Negotiate Journal*™ then you will feel better and the process *will* work.

8. If the other side is uncooperative, stick to it and **be patient**. I have been in many a mediation as a mediator in which it was **"darkest before the dawn"** and the case made a big turn for the better near the last half of the mediation.

9. I have always found it true that if a case I mediated had zero conflict/arguments and rough moments between the disputants - then the disputants were not really working on what was wrong. So **if you have rough moments in a mediation that is good.** It means you are really working on the problem.

10. Stick with it. **Trust your positivity, empathy** and respect. It WILL make a positive difference to both of you. See Chapter 8 for more about the power of empathy.

For Facilitation

1. If your facilitator doesn't request that you do this then I recommend **forming a very small group** within your business to address the problem that you plan to present to a facilitator.

Assure that all members of this group are:

1. Of sound social and mental functioning. A person who has significant mental impairment or who may pull the group off topic into tangents and side problems will *not* be a productive member of a resolution team. The team must be able to table issues and focus their energy and work on the objectives of the meetings.

♦ Are older or very mature in their interactions with others. Young inexperienced individuals do not make good members of a facilitation team, because they do not know enough about how to handle complicated problems.

Select Stable Experienced Professionals to Facilitate

♦ Have a great deal of knowledge about the dispute

♦ Include a member(s) of management who are willing to be neutral/open to alternatives

♦ Include a trusted member who will work with the team and facilitator to <u>maintain records</u> of the work.

2. **Work on your needs, wants & common interests together**. Take all the time you need. Organizational problems take a great deal of time to formulate and require a great deal of work to resolve but a good resolution will save the organization.

3. **Select a Professional Facilitator**. Meet with the Professional and get to know this person. Is this person a good fit?

♦ Do they know enough about the field/subject matter they will be taking on?

♦ Are they experienced enough in general. What I have found is to be true is the best facilitators have had some significant time on the job – they are usually older and have had a wide variety of good experience in conflict resolution.

♦ It is best if they come with a credential. Meaning that they are licensed or certified by a state board or professional entity to resolve conflict in a related professional field such as mediation, law, or counseling

4. Know that facilitation takes a **concentrated collection of meetings**. These meetings will usually last all day and the entire process (depending on scheduling) can take either a couple of weeks or months.

5. The facilitator may bring his/her own "**recorder**" or the facilitator may ask that you assign a person to "record" what is being done on flip charts. This person's job is primarily to record what is said/ brainstormed or established in the meetings on these flip charts. **Keep the flip charts,** they will be an excellent record to refer back to and the facilitator will use them to help you write the action plan.

6. **The goal of Facilitation is to write an Action Plan** – which specifies for the organization who will do what and when. Dates and responsibilities, departmental changes, product and/or service changes/ personnel changes and how all of these potential aspects of an action plan will be carried are specified in an action plan.

7. Also a **follow-up date** will be assigned at the end of the Action Plan. Assure that this is done and it is set at no longer than two months from the time the action plan is written. Keep the date set in the follow up plan to check on progress and make changes. Changes are likely to be needed.

8. **You may** further go back into mini-facilitation at this time **to continue to address the resolution of the original**

problem as it changes. You've likely laid the groundwork for a tremendous positive change in your organization and these changes will be tested the most at the very beginning.

9. Do not hesitate to **build on good work well done** (and so often not done in other businesses) Hire a new facilitator if you need to – to take the organization where it needs to go. Remember, the outcome will likely affect the future success of your organization and will be well worth the time.

10. **Keep facilitation as a regular solution** to changes that face your business or organization.

For Arbitration

1. Write/complete your *Negotiate Journal*™ and **seek legal information/representation**.

2. **Attempt to resolve the issue** with the business or other entity **outside of arbitration first.** This may save your relationship with them if this is important to you.

3. **Consult with an Attorney** or Hire an Attorney if your case involves significant money or property value. See my guide above for criteria for hiring an attorney earlier in this chapter and in chapter five.

4. **Be respectful** when in front of the arbitrator. An arbitrator is given the respect of a judge.

5. If you do not like the outcome of the case then **seek advisement from an attorney.**

For Victim's Advocacy:

1. Write/complete your *Negotiate Journal*™ Please take all the time you need and **assure to respect your needs and wants.**

2. **Seek a counselor** to help you through what you've experienced. You, I, or Anyone would do the same if any of us found ourselves in a position in which someone had abused us or endangered our very safety and survival.

3. Share your *Negotiation* **Journal™** with Your Counselor and Victim's Advocate. **They will help you to write more** and be very pleased that you are writing this.

4. **Stick with the Plan** that your victim's advocate and counselor have. Hopefully, you have both and all of you are on the same page.

5. **Seek legal help** in your area. Your victim's advocate should be able to assist you to find help if you do not have the income to choose an attorney privately.

6. **Surround yourself with supportive people** who will help you and care about you. As I stated earlier (Counseling section) only talk about positive things with other people. Keep any negative aspects of your life private.

7. Re-read my section on obtaining counseling. Counseling is like taking medicine for a cold. It keeps a person healthy and healthy is always good. **Stay in counseling** until you know you are strong enough to stand on your own with your good support system firmly in place around you and you feel safe.

Matching the EXAMPLE to a Profession

Here are examples and which professions best address them:

EXAMPLE A:

Dispute with a boss or employer

PROFESSION(S) That May Apply:

1. Human Resources (Prior to separation from your job
2. EAP Counselor
3. Attorney

WHY:

Save the relationship with your boss at all costs. Their perspective of you will follow you for a long time. Seek some outside guidance from another professional like an EAP Counselor (which is provided for free in some work locations). It would be worth your time and money to consult with a good employee counselor to help you sort through the situation if it is serious enough. Find someone who knows your specific industry. Also, an attorney could give you answers to any legal questions or issues. Do all of these things before you say or do anything to jeopardize your job.

⇒ If there has been a conflict, stop. Conflict on the job site is always bad for everyone. Don't lose your job. Choose to walk out positively when you have another job waiting and have given them adequate notice. If a crisis happens, always seek outside consultation with someone older and with the knowledge of your industry and avoid a public confrontation.

Find your voice (as I discussed in chapter one) at home on your own time. Work it out if you can. If you see that you aren't able to, keep working well on the job and seeking a better position for you so you can give notice and leave. If you do this, you will be glad you did. You will feel better about yourself for being the bigger person and others will speak highly of you after you leave because of the way you conducted yourself. See my specific help suggestions in Chapter 7 if and when you next talk to the boss.

EXAMPLE B:

Dispute with a live in or married spouse - prior to divorce or separation proceedings

PROFESSION(S) That May Apply:

1. Counseling
2. Mediation

WHY:

Counseling can help you solve the problem and/or work through the intangible aspects of it. Mediation will help you work out a separation agreement that includes the depth of your experiences together.

⇒ First, remember to find your voice using the 10-step guide. In mediation you are negotiating your side with the mediator. In counseling you will use your voice to work through the issues you face.

⇒ All of the same attributes that make up a formal dispute start first in a set of conflicts that you have with yourself *and* are compounded by the conflict you have with the other person simultaneously.

Do the work to find your voice and you will discover the best way through the conflict whether you proceed to separation and divorce or choose to reconcile.

EXAMPLE C:

Dispute with a Co-Worker or Person that is Displaying Their own Internal Conflict
(In a circumstance where the issue *must* be and can be resolved)

PROFESSION(S) That May Apply:
1. Human Resources (HR)
2. EAP Counselor
3. Negotiation or Mediation

WHY:

Talking to a friend about this could help but likely they will just say what you want to hear. Sometimes our friends can be such lifesavers when we face conflicts. Sometimes, they can worsen a situation. because they may influence you to do things that could ultimately come back to haunt you.

⇒ If you work for a larger company, an EAP Counselor may also be available to you to talk with in confidence.

If you can seek council outside of company management first, that is best.

⇒ If this is a co-worker that you must interact with, approach your HR Department for council and documentation of what is happening. If it is your boss, be careful. This may not be the place you want to work but you do not want a bad recommendation when/if you leave. If you do not feel you will be supported, start searching for another place to work and end it well.

If it is a dispute you must resolve alone, then do your "Find your voice" work (chapter 2) and seek out a supportive person in authority and begin a healthy resolution process. See Chapter 7 for guides on how to discuss a dispute with both a co-worker and boss.

⇒ Finally, if your dispute is serious enough and both you and the employer have a great deal to lose by not resolving this conflict, seek either a negotiator or mediator. An attorney could negotiate for you, or you may hire a specially trained negotiator that knows your job field well.

EXAMPLE D

Separation from Spouse

PROFESSION(S) That May Apply:
1. Counseling
2. Mediation
3. Attorney Representation

WHY & WHEN:

If you are at the beginning of a separation with your spouse, first go to counseling. Even if you decide to separate, counseling affords you the opportunity to resolve the pain and intangible issues better. As I have stated, is a better use of your money, time and energy when you go to a counselor that gives you both equal respect and helps you work out the deeper aspects of the relationship that will inevitably be present.

If you are in the middle of a separation, you are better served if you choose a mediator to resolve the settlement aspect of the dispute and use a counselor (separate appointments) to help you resolve the emotional aspects. It is time & money well spent.

If you go straight to an attorney and spill out all of what is happening and has happened you will expend large amounts of money and time and waste your energy.

⇒ Couples counseling or individual counseling will really help you both to resolve deep painful issues and this dramatic change in your life circumstances.

You will need to consult an attorney to answer legal questions. Use mediation to write out your formal agreement with or without attorneys present. I advise you to work through the toughest legal issues with your mediator. Your mediated agreement is a legal document.

⇒ Focus the time you spend with your attorney and you will have a much less stressful experience.

EXAMPLE E

Negotiation of Original Salary or New Job Contract

PROFESSION(S) That May Apply:
1. None
2. Attorney Consultant in the Job Field
3. Negotiator

If you are negotiating for new job with a salary range under $100K, then do *not* consider hiring a negotiator. Do your research in this job field and come to the discussion about salary prepared (if there is the possibility that you could make more.)

⇒ Many jobs have set salary ranges. I advise you to know these salary ranges in advance.

⇒ If you're potential job includes a specific clause that needs to be negotiated, then **do your homework on what others make in these circumstances**. An example may include a *safety clause* on the job. Another example would be a job that pays $10K for one engagement.

In these circumstances, a negotiator is probably *not* needed.

❖ If a contract involves large amounts of cumulative money ($30K+) consult an attorney in this job field.

If you are considering taking a job with a professional sport team, movie production or other large business contract over $100K or relevant amount then consider hiring either a professional negotiator or lawyer in that job field to help you.

⇒ Negotiate the best salary that your education, credentials, experience, reputation and background qualify you for.

If you are in a job already and are considering negotiating your salary know that this is often not a successful endeavor unless you have completed some years of outstanding work or landed the company significant income.

If you have been a great financial asset to this company and you have not been compensated for this, then do your research on what others are being paid in similar circumstances.

If your un-compensated work for this company is significant enough, consult an attorney who specializes in salary negotiation and work to present your case to your employer first. You may be able to negotiate a good settlement. Write/complete an *Negotiate Journal*™ for your position. Whether you decide to go to lawsuit or resolve it with the company, the *Negotiate Strategy* you create when completing the worksheet will help you in any potential negotiation or lawsuit.

FINAL EXAMPLE

Automobile or Personal Injury Claim

PROFESSION(S) That May Apply:

1. Attorney

WHY

If you have a significant claim and/or injury it is worth your time to speak to an attorney in a free consultation. Attorneys who specialize in this field are excellent in knowing whether you have a case to bring. If you do, they will negotiate your case best with the insurance company.

As a mediator, I have sat through many court cases that did *not* settle, and usually, the disputants got less compensation when they did not trust their attorney to settle. I have also sat through settlement meetings between attorneys and insurance companies.

This is the one area of ADR in which I have seen that it may be best that you, the client, allow your attorney to get the best settlement he/she can in private. It depends on your case, but your attorney is working for money and he/she will do their best.

CHAPTER 7

Negotiation in the Business Setting

My Mother Once Told Me...In this world
You must be oh so smar
or oh so pleasant
I recommend pleasan

Harvey, Original Stage Script
by Mary Chase

Respond to Business Disputes Differently

If you wish to negotiate in the business setting then the approach is different. You may need to recommend that your client write/complete a ***Negotiate Journal™*** if the dispute is impacting his/her job or income.

In the business setting, the ***Negotiate Journal™*** is used differently. A client writes it, then puts it away. Consider their perspective *and* the other side's perspective deeply. Then, consider the following acronym to prepare your client before he/she speaks again with business officials or co-workers:

P – Prepare Yourself to
A – Act /Speak with
C – Consistency &
E – Efficiency

P.A.C.E. is an acronym that I created for another book series (scheduled to come out in the summer of 2014) to help professionals and first responders who deal with crisis. I believe it applies here for a separate but related set of reasons. When you face disputes and conflicts in a business setting it feels like a crisis very quickly because of *where* you are experiencing the dispute and because those you experience the dispute/conflict *with* are members of your work life and not your personal life.

If you work with individuals who are also your family members or personal friends outside of work – then – in times of conflict use the ***Negotiate Journal*™** for in dispute resolution. To stop and take the time to write this down will help you to P.A.C.E. yourself to resolve issues that arise.

Learning The P.A.C.E. - - Suggested Statements for Your Clients

Prepare to Act with Consistency & Efficiency

At work when you face a dispute:

❖ **Stop, take a deep breath, and find a reason to take a brief moment *away*** from the situation. *Grab a quick cold beverage or take a moment to visit the restroom.* It will give you and the other person the moment to think and react better.

❖ **Don't Leave & Text someone or Eat**. Don't call anyone or check your messages. This is disrespectful and will inflame the situation. You can take a sip from a beverage; most people would give you a *pass* for this, as it denotes that you're trying to cool down.

In the moments you are away from the situation:

❖ **Push *Your* Reset Button**. Even if you've had an argument with this person before or you are presently in an argument with this person now, don't feel that you have to return to it.

⇒ Think of it as a mistake you made in a marathon of running too fast for a while. When you get that first breather, resolve to reset yourself into a new pace that is going to successfully complete this objective. **The objective is to maintain this working relationship** with a positive conclusion to this particular point or working situation.

These guidelines apply to all business conflicts. Business conflicts are different because **you do not want to go into your deeper emotional feelings**. It is not the right environment to do this.

In the movies, a great deal of drama and melodrama happens in work place settings. This works in the movies because story lines are designed to represent larger societal motif's to please the audience.

> ⇒ In real life it is not appropriate to talk about your deeper emotional needs in the work setting. It is best to learn how to ask for what you need respectfully and respond respectfully to others.

If arguments happen, let them go. Let all of your past anger, frustration, jealousy and negativity go. It will help *you* and your *career* to do this.

ᶠ you are reading this book from beginning to end, you may find ᵗ at some of the directives in this chapter are similar. This is ᵉcause **all conflicts require some of the same steps** to ˉstematically deal with problems. I decided it was better for me to ave steps *in* rather than take them out and set readers up for ˉᵢitting very important objectives to success.

Quick note about myself: *I am a member of a very well established family business. I have worked in every single aspect of my family's business. During my years as a licensed counselor, I spent several years as an employee counselor, business mediator and facilitator.*

Co-Worker / Co-Worker Disputes

Stop Using Traditional Methods That Do Not Work

When you have a dispute **with a co-worker or individual who is at the same level** of employment status as you (you're both supervisors, department heads, or on nearly the same status level at your work site) then first accept that you both are equal.

This person deserves your respect no matter what your feelings are about their personal or professional choices. They likely annoy you and you disagree with a great deal about how they do their job.

Even if you respect this person and you both just disagree on something *still* use this guide.

I've begun the process above with setting your mind on PACE.

These Steps BELOW Apply in
　　Any *One on One* Dispute at the Same Level

In An Argument or Before One Starts

1. Stop & Take a Break
2. Give a good reason – *restroom/ cold beverage*
3. Come back to the situation and Ask **"What do *you* think?" "I really do want to understand your perspective."**
4. Allow them to talk. When/If they ask you the same.
5. Respond by first **complimenting this person on something you *genuinely* like that they did.**
6. Then very simply and succinctly **give them your opposing opinion and offer another option.**

7. **Ask what they think** about the other option
8. If the response is positive, then very slowly enter into **2 -3 more exchanges** if the conversation is positive and
9. **Bring the conversation to a positive close**
10. Back in your own private space or desk, **make note of the positive things that happened** and what you learned. Bring these into your next conversation with this person.

If the conversation goes badly

From either point above (#4 on *or* #6 on) then say:

1. **"I understand how you came to that conclusion or why you think that."**
2. STOP
3. Do not try and convince the other person that you are right and that they are wrong. **Do not justify your position.** Do not give them a long history of the problem that shows how you are right. Just stop.

4. Pause and nod your head. You're not nodding in agreement **you are nodding that you understand as you listen** and do not interrupt.

Consider Their Perspective, There may be Points of Value

5. Consider their perspective. Continue to remain silent or only say one or two words that are positive – indicating that you hear them.
6. If they ask you to respond (*seeming to instigate a fight*) do not take the bait. Just say: **"I am taking a moment to hear you and understand."**

7. **End the conversation well**.

8. You do not have to agree with someone to work with him/her or even like this person. **It may be an issue that can just drop. If it is. Drop it. Move on.**

9. If the problem must be dealt with beyond your disagreement, then very quietly and not in a blaming way, go to your supervisor and very objectively let him/her know that the two of you simply disagree. **Do not make the other person wrong or try and place yourself in a favorable position no matter how much you may think that you need to.** Your HR person &/or Supervisor will see right through you and likely this will hurt your standing with them.

10. It will be much more beneficial to you to **honestly talk to your supervisor** and let them know that **you want to do everything you can to work it out**.

Co-Worker / Supervisor

In these disputes there is **a power imbalance**. The supervisor has power over the employee and therefore the conversation is really not about collaboration. Since **the supervisor has the power to fire you or give you a poor mark on a job performance**, it is up to the employee to **survive** and get through the dispute by respecting the supervisor.

Never fight with a supervisor. If some person is going to be physically harmed then you may step in and prevent harm. If an injustice is happening, then go to the supervisor and pose the discussion this way:

1. **"Thank you for making a few moments to talk with me about___"**
2. Be as brief and specific as you can. The night before or the week before take some time and think carefully about how to **say the least amount of words as possible.**
3. **Use only positive words and phrases.**
4. Present your problem in 1 – 3 sentences.
5. Avoid bringing in any other co-worker into the situation to "make your case stronger" when you are presenting the

problem. **Just present this from your perspective only.**

6. Stop. **Listen respectfully** to the response you get. **Do not interrupt.**
7. **Summarize** what they have told you very positively and briefly.
8. Do no rant and rave. Do not go into a long story. If you are asked to tell your story, make the story as brief as possible.
9. Stop.
10. Say, **"I need some time to think on this."**
11. **Thank the supervisor** for their time that they gave you.
12. **Leave the situation positively** and return to work.

If you are dealing with a supervisor who continues to pick and pick, just continue to respectfully say, **"I need to take some time to think on what you've told me to do."**

If your supervisor does not offer you any advisement, then just say **"Thank you for making some time to talk to me. I appreciate your leadership. I will go back to work now and consider how I can make this better on my end."** Use specifics from your work environment.

Bad Bosses

Many supervisors out there don't know how to resolve conflicts. Many don't know how to be supervisors. You must let go of your frustration about this. All you can do is talk to them and talking to them positively is a good step in the right direction.

If you keep what you have to say positive, then when you look back on the conversation, you will be glad you did.

> ⇒ If you are in a situation that does not resolve itself in a few weeks, then talk to your Human Resources Manager. If you don't have this opportunity then you must think deeply about this situation. **Is it worth risking your job?** Should you look for employment somewhere else?

Consider going to the next level of supervision if you feel it is worth the risk and you must. **Use the exact same guidelines (co-worker/supervisor) with even more respect.**

> ⇒ Remember to **avoid blaming anyone** and re-state that **you want to do all that you can to help resolve this**

issue and **request that the conversation remain confidential**. It may *not* remain confidential, but if you feel it is worth the risk, then do what you need to do to help resolve the problem. You may simultaneously want to look for another place of employment because if the problem persists and is *this* bad then you would want to work in an environment that is not so stressful.

Supervisor / Employee

Any person in a supervisory position between employees below and management above will need to practice conflict resolution skills, because one of your job responsibilities will be to resolve disputes.

If you are a supervisor, likely you are a type A personality, meaning that you are ambitious and work very hard.

Build Good Working Relationships

If you haven't also developed the skills you need to turn off the "high" lever on your work personality let me first encourage you to **find out where you "high" and "low" switches are inside** yourself.

When an employee comes to talk to you or if you need to go to an employee or management, you will need to **switch your internal work mode to "low." Reset your P.A.C.E.** Prepare yourself to make brief positive statements and to slow down and think before you respond.

Employees are going to come to you in conflict and ask you for answers. **Take some time to formulate your responses.** Take a break and consider what you will say. Cool drinks – always cool down situations: grab both of you one. Feel free to comfort the employee and let them know that you will come back to them tomorrow with more specific steps.

❖ Deliver all steps, responses, statements and directives to an employee with the utmost respect.

Thank the employee for specific aspects of what he/she is doing well.

Keep your word and return to talk to the employee
Keep the conversation private and the fact that the meeting occurred confidential

If you must make notes in a personnel file, then consult your manager or HR director about the best way to do this before writing anything down.

Supervisor / Employee

Delivering A Reprimand or Negative Feedback

1. **"Thank you for coming in to talk with me about___ "**
2. Be as brief and specific as you can.
3. First tell the employee **how much you appreciate the fine work he/she has done in 1-3 specific areas** _____,
   _____, _____.
4. Present the problem or issue **in one sentence.** Keep it simple. Do not go into multiple issues. One problem at a time.
5. Ask them how they feel about this. Give them plenty of time to respond. Encourage them to tell you their side. **Listen respectfully** to the response you get. **Do not interrupt.**
6. **Summarize** what they have told you very positively and briefly.

7. **Ask them if they have any suggestions**.

8. Listen carefully. You may learn something very valuable from this employee. **People usually have problems with objectives that may need some adjustment from higher management.**

9. Say "**Thank you for the feedback you gave me. I will consider this.**"

10. Give the directive(s) you need to positively and briefly.

11. Ask, "**Do you have any questions?**" Answer these questions clearly and specifically. Take time to clear up very small details with patience.

12. Ask, "**Do you understand what needs to happen next?**"

13. Summarize positively what you've gone over and **emphasize the employee's strengths. Let them know you believe in their ability.**

14. Leave the situation positively and return to work.

15. Remember, resolutions are built like a brick foundation. Lay one solid brick at a time. **If you have a good conversation with an employee it can begin a new experience for them at work.**

The best way to avoid reprimanding employees is **to check in positively with them often.** Talk to them and reward them for doing well.

❖ Foster a good work atmosphere by bringing snacks for everyone and whenever you can, **work along side employees.** This gives you a good chance to show your leadership abilities when the opportunity arises.

Employee / Customer- Client

*For the sake of simplicity, I am going to refer to these individuals as **customers**, but this also applies to individuals in higher income businesses as well (often referred to as **clients**, **guests, patrons**...).*

❖ If a customer / client or potential client approaches you either *in* conflict or *with* a dispute about the business, stop & think before you make statements.

First know that **every person within earshot of this customer is a** ***potential*** **customer of this business.** How you handle this person will affect those potential customers and affect co-workers and your existing customer base because people talk and conflict is interesting.

So, a customer comes into your business or begins talking to you anywhere about this business in a negative way. Here is what to do:

1. Stop & **Listen for at least three minutes**. Do not interrupt.
2. If they ask you to respond, just say, **"I am listening. I want to understand."**
3. Take a moment and resolve their problem if possible.

4. Likely you didn't expect that you would have to do this. Check yourself. **It's your job to stop and resolve problems.** Just do it as politely as you can.
5. Thank the person for their business.
6. Smile genuinely. Image how *you* feel when you are frustrated.

7. If the person is doing this on purpose to try and create a bad impression in a lobby or on line or anywhere else, then it is best to simply **find a reason to quietly leave the room and get your supervisor.** Let the person have a few moments to collect himself/herself and realize the scene that they are creating.

8. It is not often that a customer will do this. If they do it is usually because they are **mad about something else or something bigger than you can solve.**

9. Come back to the person and say, **"How can _I_ best help you?"**

10. **Allow them to talk in a private area**. Listen in a caring way. Do not interrupt.
11. **Summarize** what they have asked.
12. Agree to address at least **one of the things they have asked** you and more if these things are simple and within _your_ ability to do. If not, simply tell them this politely and positively end the conversation.
13. Remember, we all "lose it" from time to time. When you "lose it" you are grateful when someone takes a few moments to help you.
14. Take a few moments to help this person if you can.
15. Get assistance respectfully from a manager or owner if you need to.

16. **Do not embarrass the person** by saying sarcastically "I NEED to GET MY _MANAGER_." This just makes the entire situation worse and your supervisor will not be pleased that you did this. You _will_ make a bad impression to everyone who hears/see you and likely lose the business of more than one customer. Remember, "the customer is always right."

17. Customers talk. **If you take a few moments to be kind and helpful to someone who is behaving badly they will appreciate this**, though they are not likely to tell you.
18. If you do _not_ take time to help them, this customer is going to talk negatively about this business and it may ultimately come back on _you_ negatively.

19. If a customer is negatively targeting the business with the objective of hurting the business, then **report them in private to the appropriate authorities** or online companies to resolve the situation privately.

20. **Offer customers who have had a bad experience a coupon for something free or another service/product at no cost**. The customer is always right, and you want them to come back another day and bring friends.

Chapter 8

Negotiating Interpersonal Conflicts:

Resolution Comes from Empathy

I've learned that people will forget what you said,

people will forget what you did, but people will

never forget how you made them feel.

Maya Angelou

Before You Talk to Your Spouse, Significant Other or Enemy STOP

If you let words fly out of your mouth about multiple subjects simultaneously– your likelihood of resolving your initial problem is greatly diminished. Do not talk about the entire problem at once. If the *other* person is doing this to *you*, then ask them if you can take a break, then start again by saying:

"I would like it if we could please talk about one small part of this at a time."

Practice saying this statement (above) silently in your mind. What ever statement you make, assure that it is respectful and caring. If you say anything sarcastically, you've blown your chance to start this communication right.

The other person you are speaking to is now intensely stressed. You've raised a problem, so if you goofed and it came out wrong, say:

"I didn't mean that to come out sarcastically and I am not trying to avoid the problem. I really want to solve this, and the best way I can do that is to talk about one small part of this at a time."

Think of resolutions like bites of a good dinner. Good meals are enjoyed one bite at a time and so are good conversations. A good conversation is all about pace and quality *not quantity* of material consumed.

Why Negotiating Multiple Issues at Once Doesn't Work

Building a good *negotiation* is like building a brick house. You **don't slap on multiple bricks at a time; you lay them one at a time and allow one layer of foundation to set up** well before building another one on top of it. When you rush the layers and issues you diminish your power to build a solid resolution.

> ❖ *If you've read the first seven chapters of my book you have read about why this is important already. It is even truer in interpersonal relationships because in a sense, all relationships are personal on some level. And, if you even remotely skip the importance of this in an intimate relationship, the entire process just degrades and is not repaired until you go back and begin it right again.*

No problem is ever about one simple thing. But you will solve many things if you take on the problem one small brick at a time and **stay in the same "layer."** Trust me. **Do not go to another issue until you solve the one you're on *well.*** If you get to an issue that needs deep research and consideration, **"table it" meaning that you do come back to it later.** Take on an even smaller issue and resolve it well.

It will empower you in more ways than one to come back to a complex or harder issue later because you will have **laid a foundation for resolving it well.** If you've ever been in an argument with a personal friend or family member, you know that in arguments multiple issues fly up and against one another in a chaos of disrespect, talking over, anger.... All this does is make every situation worse.

START

Begin a negotiation by **selecting an issue that is small and solvable.** Once you begin, you will realize that this issue is harder than you thought. Expect this. Allow the small issue to carry the emotional weight of the larger problem because it IS solvable.

NEGOTIATING FINANCIAL ISSUES

Let's say for example, a couple is arguing over who spends more money. This is actually a compound issue.

With a Familiar Yet Business Approach

To negotiate this *well* they may begin by:

    A. Choosing to discuss how and when to pay their gasoline bill for their cars. Or

    B. They could choose another single bill that has less significance to it if possible. Choosing a bill to negotiate that is relatively fixed leaves room for less opportunity to go off topic into another discussion.

Negotiate Interpersonal Financial Issues

If you think this may bring up a very compound issue like "should we sell your vehicle or mine" then do not start with that bill. Take a complicated bill after you have successfully negotiated a simpler bill. See how this works?

Negotiate how this bill will be paid using the ground rules.

GROUND RULES of NEGOTIATING/TALKING With EACH OTHER

FIRST: **Empathize**

Empathizing means to imagine how you would feel if the same thing happened to you.

⇒ Take into account *why* the other person feels the way they feel – and imagine that you really feel this way too. Usually people are not *trying* to be self-centered, they just want to be heard and they think you will not understand them.

⇒ Each one of us has very important reasons for the way we feel that we rarely get the opportunity to explain to you and very often people avoid talking to you about certain things because they fear what you will think.

When I teach teenagers how to understand this concept I tell them:

❖ "Imagine you just watched someone stump their toe and call out in pain. Have you ever fallen or stumped your toe? Remember how that felt?" This is what it is like to empathize. Imagine *you* are feeling what the other person is feeling while they are talking to you.

EMPATHY Applied Consistently & Well Over Time Can SAVE A Personal Relationship

Sympathy is feeling sorry for someone. It is not the same thing as empathy. **Empathy** is imaging *yourself* feeling mad, frustrated, sad, happy, jealous… You step into their shoes and see something from his/her point of view. The first requirement of a good friendship is the ability to empathize with one another.

The biggest reason most relationships fail is because one side or the other or <u>both</u> feel like the *other person* no longer empathizes with how he or she feels. They may not *say* the word "empathy" but this is what they really mean.

Empathy in a Romantic Relationship

If you learn to empathize with your significant other, you will know one the most important skills to making a romantic relationship work.

❖ There also is an expectation that you will **take this empathy a step further**. Your significant other expects you to **become a member of his/her "team."** All spouses have an unspoken expectation that their significant other is "on their side." He or She expects you to empathize with his/her perspective.

This means – instead of telling him/her how he/she is wrong or could do this better – to empathize – you would say – **"I understand why you feel that way. I would feel that way too."**

DO NOT say the word BUT. **When you say "but" it cancels out every single thing that you said before.** It erases all of your patient work that you did to show that you cared about this person. Accept what they have told you. Say something else positive and end this conversation there on a positive note.

SECOND: Change the Way You Approach a Discussion with the Other Person

Instead of returning to a *My* Way / *Your* Way argument, do something entirely different. Take a break and relax. Talk a walk somewhere peaceful. Open your heart and mind and come back together.

❖ Agree that when you come back you will **take turns talking without interruption** and that each of you will listen and take time to hear what the other person is saying and try and feel what they are feeling. This is called setting healthy boundaries with someone.

Let's say a man and wife are arguing over her bills for clothes and shoes. He does not understand why she needs to spend so much. He and she take a break and agree to the terms of respect above and they come back together in a little while. Relaxed, he asks her how wearing beautiful clothes makes her feel and he learns **to empathize with her** as he listens. If the wife in turn gives him the exact same respect over an issue she formerly didn't understand/agree with – then you've both taken a positive step toward a new way of interacting.

THIRD: Remind Yourself That the Way You Were Arguing Was Not Working

To fall right back into a bad pattern is such a strong instinct that I've made it an OBJECTIVE for you to REMIND YOURSELF: It Doesn't Work

The way most people "negotiate" is to:

❖ Let the other person talk, then show him/her how he/ she is wrong.

This path has not led you to success. It is the continuation of an argument in which *neither* of you will win or accomplish anything.

FOURTH: Whenever You Hit A Wall and Begin to Argue, Stop & LISTEN Again

Stop negotiating for a while and take some time to listen with caring to each other and no expectations. This happens so frequently in interpersonal relationships. Don't give up. Listening is powerful.

❖ The act of caring for someone and listening to their feelings, their journey without expectation or interruption is what the other person needs.

❖ To do this changes the argument into a something much more powerful and important that will help give you the confidence to negotiate again later.

We all need someone to listen to us and care about us. **Each spouse expects this of the other**, whether they say that or not, and **interpersonal friends and co-workers silently wish this as well.** When we take the time to listen to someone, we give him/her what he/she needs.

FIFTH: **The Only Person You Can Change is *You***

Free yourselves from the expectation that you can change the other person or the situation. You cannot change people unless you use force. Force creates internal violence within both the person being forced and the person forcing someone. Both are bad and begin a new cycle of violence (Hope, 2009; 2014) between the two of you.

❖ Change yourself. Change your responses from long statements of anger to clear, respectful responses that are supportive and positive. You will instantly feel better and you will immediately change the entire tone of the conversation.

REACTIONS IN A CONFLICT

You Have Three Choices in Any Exchange of Communication

Verbal, Written, Sign Language, or powerful *Look* in someone's direction, you can do one of three things:

1. Nothing or Give a blank face;

2. Shout, Bully or Say or Do Something Sarcastic,

3. Say or Do Something Genuinely Positive

This is how these reactions play out....

1. **Nothing** – avoid the problem/issue/argument.

If you choose to do this to diffuse an argument, in the moment, this is a good choice.

If you choose to continuously do nothing and not deal with a problem your problem/issue or argument is likely to intensify. When it finally manifests itself it will be worse, because not dealing with it caused negativity to build in the other person and maybe in you as well.

❖ A conflict that was once over *one* thing is now over several *other* things as well because your anger/sadness/ or other negative feelings make other issues *seem* even worse than they may actually be. Then the original issue becomes that much more difficult to solve.

The only reason to ignore or avoid dealing with an issue or problem is to give yourself the appropriate amount of time to think of the best way to handle that issue positively and with respect to both your own needs and the needs of the other person.

2. **Negatively Say What you Feel** to the other person, regardless of whether it is the best way to confront the issue.

This will always lead to a multidimensional conflict.

a. You will be in conflict with yourself. You will feel bad about yourself for dealing with this poorly at some point in the near future.

b. You will stimulate a negative conflict inside the feelings of the other person.

c. You will worsen the entire situation.

Also, it is important to note here that if you smile but you really are *not* saying something positive or you mix any amount of negative or perceived negative in your statement or response – it comes across as negative and thereby counts as negative.

❖ **The judge here is the person who *receives* your communication.**

❖ If you goof or somehow don't communicate what you want to say *well* – then keep working on it. Adapt what you say to be respectful and really say what you mean. If there is some negativity in you – then there is something you are not being honest with yourself about and likely this is being communicated to the other person.

It also could be that *they* are not hearing what they need to – to believe you.

If it's *their* perception – it may be based on how they've heard things in the past. If you care about this person, say what *they* need to hear. For instance, if they need to hear you say, "I'll do *this* _____ for you every Tuesday..." If you are truly ok with what you are communicating and have no internal conflicts, you will easily just adapt and say what they need to hear that is genuinely true.

❖ If you have a problem with restating something, then time to look deeper inside. They may be sensing something you aren't aware of. We all have internal conflicts and often it is others that see them for us and help us realize it. This is a gift to us. This is the only real way we know sometimes that we have internal pain and issues that we didn't realize.

3. **Positively State What you Feel** to the other person.

When you do this, you are negotiating your position. It doesn't mean this is the right answer or best answer, it is simply *you* stating positively how *you* really feel and what you want to say in a way that respects both you and the other person.

❖ It usually takes time to **develop a good set of statements that negotiate your position well.** Sometimes, you don't have the time to do this in the moment that the issue arises – and you may falter and state your position poorly. This doesn't mean that you decide *not* to negotiate.

❖ What you must do then is take time to consider the entire situation. Search for the best thing to say. You know what has happened and your potential to resolve it best. Believe in yourself. You *can* negotiate difficult emotional issues well if you **make short simple statements** that respect the other person.

NEGOTIATING HURT FEELINGS

If YOU'VE hurt someone's feelings and you want to make amends for this:

Begin by expecting the conversation to either be a long one or come back later for final resolution

1. Ask the other person if they will make some time to talk to you.
2. Say to the other person, **"I believe I messed up. I want to apologize to you because I believe I have hurt you." "I want to give you the opportunity to talk to me about how you feel."**
3. **Specify** an easier **or smaller aspect of the situation** (*if the issue is complicated*) then allow them to talk about how they feel.

4. **Listen. Do not interrupt**. Do not argue back or present your point of view. Do not tell them why. Do not justify your behavior. Listen and accept what they have to say.
5. The other person has a right to their feelings and **if you genuinely allow them the respect of being hurt** and more specifically *angry* or frustrated about specific parts of the situation, **then you slowly free them of the pain of it.**

6. You justifying your behavior will not free them. It will make it worse.

7. Accept every single aspect of what they have to say and **allow them to continue to talk**. If they ask *you* to talk, do

not start talking about how you feel *yet*. Just encourage them to continue until you know that they are finished.

8. **Be very supportive.** Take a break. Hug the person and thank them for telling you how they feel. End the conversation so you both can give yourselves time to let this hurt go.

9. If you want or need to talk about *your* side of this – that is completely healthy and fine. I recommend **making a time the next day or in a few days** to do this. Do it soon; do not let weeks or longer go by because your relationship with this individual is important. **Give it the priority it deserves**.

10. Continue to be supportive and kind to the person you have hurt after this. You will be **building a foundation for a new relationship** with this person that is positive. Sometimes, the best friends are those who were former enemies that worked through something very difficult well.

If Someone Has Hurt *Your* Feelings and *You* Need to Talk to Them About It:

1. Ask the person if they will **make time in one afternoon** to talk with you. Afternoons are usually a good time. Individuals are often in the highest part of their energy. This way they will have completed their morning objectives and they will have the evening to give time to your conversation.

2. Let the person know that this may take awhile, offer to **meet them for coffee**, late lunch, or a dessert. A meeting over a bite to eat helps. Be flexible. No matter where you've decided to meet, assure both of you have access to something to drink and to a nice restroom because it is a good to hydrate in awkward moments.

3. When they are present, let the person first know that you **appreciate them making time for you**. Assure that your

thank you is genuine. It will help this discussion to begin by genuinely thanking them.

4.   Start the discussion by saying, **"First I want you to know that since I've known you, you've done _____, (1 – 3 things) that I have enjoyed sharing with you** and *"there is no but after this sentence." I like this about you period."* You want to say something about your relationship that is true and that is positive about the time you have shared. Don't say "but" after that. "But" negates what you said. Best to take a break after this and order food, or talk about a good time you've shared.

5.   Don't start a phone call or send a text. This is disrespectful. **Turn the sound off on your phone** and do not take calls or text during your conversation.

6.   Come back from this very brief break and say, **"I need to tell you how I feel about something."**

7.   **"When this situation.... occurred, you did ____ and it hurt me."**

8.   **"I know you may not have meant to hurt me, but you did."**

9.   Pause. Do not say anything further. You've just ripped the band-aid off. Do not dig open the wound. Best to simply say that and stop. If you feel sad, cry. You do not have to be melodramatic, just allow yourself to feel the feelings.

10.   Likely this person will apologize. If they do, **accept their apology by saying so**.

11.   When you are ready then say, **"This is how I would like you treat me... or what I would like you to do *instead* in the future...."** Be very specific, clear and brief.

12.   Hopefully, the other person will not interrupt you and defend themselves, argue, blame, or justify their behavior. If they do. **Let them say what they need to say**. Do not respond. Do not defend yourself or justify your feelings. To do this will not be productive for either of you.

13.   Simply remain silent for a brief moment. **Give yourself the respect you need. You have a right to have feelings and**

let someone know if they hurt you if you want to continue in a relationship with this person. If this person is relatively healthy they will soon stop arguing/blaming justifying and realize this.

14. If things get ugly. Take a brief restroom break and come back. **Sometimes, it will be best to be silent** and simply let them talk and you listen without interrupting or making what they have to say "wrong."

15. If you want to remain in a relationship with this person, then before this conversation ends you will next say "**I know we can get beyond this.**" Or something to this effect. You can also say "**I care about you. I know you care about me and you did not mean to hurt me.**"

16. Then say, "**Thank you for giving me this opportunity to talk to you. You mean a lot to me. I want to work through this.**"

17. Lastly, you can and should set a date to **spend time with this person again** within the week. If it is your spouse/ or significant other that you live with then make a date to do something you both enjoy within that week that is very positive.

18. Also if you live with this person **go out for dinner** that evening.

19. **If you want to end your relationship** with this person, then end the conversation at #16.

20. If you end it, then stick to your guns. Refrain from talking negatively about this person. Remember, they know you well and old conflicts can come back to haunt you if you don't resolve them well. You can only control your own actions, and **you *can* be respectful to someone who has hurt you. You've just given yourself the respect you**

needed. Let some time pass. Keep things positive about this conflict in the future. If they come back to you with a similar hurt, then listen and give them the same respect.

Why Do People Hurt One Another

The short answer is they usually don' intend to, but people hurt those close to them because they mistakenly feel like it should be all right to lash out a someone they've shown love and trus to. This is the wrong thing to do, but is often that I have experienced this a true.

You *Want Y*our Relationship to Be Touchy/Feely

It is never all right to hurt someone.

*People have arguments MOSTLY because they have **lost touch** with one another **emotionally**.*

Our emotions are what make us human and we expect those we've chosen to be intimate with to care about us. Note I used the word "intimate" and not "sex." These are two separate things. Some people (more often males) separate the act of sex as different from intimacy. Intimacy means to have a love relationship with someone. Some individuals (more often females) equate sex as the same as intimacy. These are important separate side topics, so assure that you both are on the same page about whether you have an intimate relationship. When both feel that the relationship is or should be intimate, what I have to advise you applies.

If you don't care about the other person, or remind yourself that this other person you are intimate with needs care and empathy, then you will just keep on pounding away to get your way and you may disregard what I have to say and label it "touchy feely."

If you feel yourself labeling the techniques I am giving you as "touchy feely" then remember my analogy at the beginning of chapter two about the pigs running off a cliff.

Just because everyone else says something…. doesn't make it is true or the right way to think about something. This book is specifically targeted to help humans deal with vague issues of emotional conflict. Labeling it as "touchy feely" will send you right over the cliff with the rest of the pigs in ignorance.

You WANT Your Romantic Relationships to be "Touchy Feely"

Think about it.

Touchy/feely on the *outside* comes from good touchy feely on the *inside* first.

- ❖ If you didn't have these invisible emotions inside you – you would belong to a different animal species. **Our Emotions and Our Ability to Talk About How We Feel** are one of the main sets of traits that separate us as human from all other animal species on the earth.

- ❖ If you are not able to empathize with how another person feels, it is likely because someone has not or did not love you enough in this specific area in your past.

UNIVERSAL TRUTH ABOUT ALL CONFLICTS

Any situation that you may need to negotiate is always:
- 90% or more about the past
- Exists because of a lack of knowledge and/or
- Exists because of a *perception* that there is a lack of caring.

All of these states of being are 100% repairable - if you take the steps to save your relationship.

The trusted methods of finding common needs and interests work. To resolve the emotional aspects of the problem, you will need to step back and **show the other human(s) involved that you really *do* care** and understand their perspective.

*Perception **is** reality to the person perceiving it. Each person's perception is equally valid.*

What if you do not understand or agree with their perspective?

1. Even if you do not agree, **you are capable of understanding** the other person's perspective. Take time and listen to them without interrupting them or trying to make *your* perspective *their* perspective.

2. **If you do not agree, then accept the difference** and find a more mature side of *yourself* that accepts the other perspective even though you do not agree with it.

Denial

Often, people say that they have done one or more of the things above, when in reality they have not. They are in denial.

⇒ When you are in **denial**, you don't know it. When everyone else around you is shaking his/her head while listening to you, it's your first clue that there is an inconsistency somewhere – which usually indicates that you're *not* dealing with something. Individuals are in denial **when they do not know how to deal with something and/or do not recognize that there is a problem**.

⇒ When you have begun a path to resolve something *well*, you know it.

OVERCOMING Denial – Find the Humiliating Truth

⇒ After you begin to face it, you realize it wasn't that bad.

⇒ Then you will have the strength to begin to do something new.

When you are 100 percent certain that you are on a long path toward success and are doing the hard work to resolving something difficult…Then you do not see progress. In my opinion, you are *still* in denial about something else.

⇒ You will need to go back and re-examine things. **Find the humiliating truth about your own behavior.**

Likely, you are stuck in a bad tradition of trying to establish what is "right" as being something "universal". **It is never that easy nor is it finite.** Focus on your own behavior for a while. It is healthy to recognize that something could be better about who you are and how you approach things.

RECOGNIZING INTERNAL CONFLICT IN *YOURSELF*

When you hurt someone else….That is *your* internal conflict rearing its ugly head.

This is not something you realize in the moment it happens, because more often, you are caught up in the emotions that caused the outburst.

"It's because of *that* or *this*…" we say to ourselves.

But it's really because of our *own* unresolved issue. Yes, what ever *that* was that we lash out about – *is* important. What is more important is what is unresolved in us that made us lash out. Ask yourself:

⇒ "What is preventing me from pausing and saying something positive or taking a moment to just stop talking?"

NORMAL Childhood Development

Children have many outbursts. This is a normal part of development and children need love and repetitive guidance to learn positive ways of responding to things. So the next time you see a child flipping out, cut the parent and kid some slack – outbursts are normal for children.

Children usually grow out of these emotional outbursts when they have positive, loving parenting and supportive environments in which they feel safe and have their basic needs taken care of. Learning these lessons of healthy emotional response take many years of time and a great deal of patience, repetition and persistence from loving, battle-scarred parents.

It is not easy parenting children to learn to control their impulses. **Neither is it easy for adults to learn to develop their emotional intelligence**. Keep working on it. You will be able to respond positively. Do not expect to be perfect, just expect to keep working to get it right, then even more right.

Childhood that Lacked Good Emotional Support

If you are a person who has not had the benefit of love, safety, and your basic survival needs being met, anyone can understand why you would have trouble with conflicts in your life. **This is no excuse.**

*If this has been your background, then **do not deny it**.* Accept it and **find love in the world *before* you negotiate volatile feelings**. Read my "couple of tips" below about "having trouble in most relationships."

It is healthy and good to find loving and supportive people to surround yourself with and **put distance between you and people who constantly make you feel like you are not good.**

Coping with This Past As An Adult

You don't have to express ugly feelings toward those who have hurt you. You will feel better if you don't. You do have to put distance in time and space between you and those who make you feel like you are not good. **You can find people who will care about you. Go out into the world and be nice and kind to others.** They will begin to be nice to you and you will be able to find friends.

IF YOU'RE HAVING TROUBLE IN MOST OF YOUR PERSONAL RELATIONSHIPS

Here are a couple of tips I have recommended many times that have been successful. I've also used these in my own life when times got tough.

1. Start doing good things for other people (*or for your significant other*) and do not expect anything in return. Soon you will begin to feel love and appreciation from those *you* do good for. Do not expect this at first; they won't know to show you this at first. After awhile, they will.

    ⇒ Allow the caring and love you feel from others to sink in and keep it going.

    ⇒ After awhile, you will realize you have made friends and/or strengthened your primary relationship. When others begin to seek *you* out – just to say hello and inquire about how you are this is a clear sign that they care about you.

    ⇒ Go out and do things with your friends. **Having friends and maintaining friendships is a crucial part of survival *and* a crucial part of being able to negotiate conflicts well.**

    ⇒ You will find others who are your true friends. They will slowly want to spend time with you, and do positive social things with you that you will like.

2. **Go to counseling** in private. It is a healthy choice. It is your own business and no one else's. It is like taking medicine for a cold.

- **Counseling can tremendously help you change your entire life if you truly *do* commit to the pain of being honest with yourself** and **take the guidance a good counselor can give you.**

3. Do positive things with a new group of friends – go out to eat, go to sporting events, comedies, social gatherings… **there are many exciting and challenging new things you can learn to challenge you that will be fun and open up a new world for you**

4. **Avoid dark, negative behavior** (dark video games, movies, cult like activities, drug use….) because these things will pull you back down. If you've had a history of neglect/abuse in your life – these things will pull out the pain inside in a bad way and you do not need to dig back into these wounds and make them worse.

If you stick with a positive group of new friends, they may eventually ask you to come into their happy and healthy environment for holidays.

5. **Go to healthy places for holidays**. It helps prevent conflicts that can grow inside of you.

You can make healthy friends. Just trust me that simply being nice to others and not expecting anything in return will eventually work out for you. Eventually, someone will say to you – "Hey, let's go grab something to eat..." and your friendship will grow from there.

6. **Don't lay heavy emotional requirements or baggage on new friends**. Just stay in the moment and enjoy what you're doing. If and when you do ever share past pain do so one small revelation at a time and don't ever share too much.

7. Stay focused in the present and leave the pain of the past behind you. Doing these things helps prevent internal conflict. **Internal conflict is the driving force behind all deep seeded conflicts.**

Negotiate

Every single one of us faces disputes, conflicts and crisis in our lives. The first step to putting conflict behind us is learning to *negotiate* **conflicts well.**

When the conflict is serious enough that a lack of resolution is going to impact your life, write/complete a *Negotiate* **Journal**™ and follow my 10 Steps using the *Negotiate Strategy*™. **This process works.**

Here's my challenge to you:

Take out paper and a pencil right now and make some time to write/complete a *Negotiate Journal* for facing a conflict or dispute. Flip back to the chapters you need. Read them again. Write down *your position* and take my advice on how to approach this conflict.

Now, go *negotiate*: resolve it right this time.

Bibliography

FOR EVERYONE:

That's Not What I Meant: How Conversational Style Makes or Breaks Relationships
Tannen, D. (2011,1992,1986). New York: Harper Perennial; Rei Rep edition. Original publisher Ballantine Books

How To Make Meetings Work: The New Interaction Method
Doyle, M., & Straus, D. (1993; 1976). New York: Berkley Trade.

Making Peace: A Guide to Overcoming Church Conflict
Van Yperen, J. (2002). Chicago: Moody Publishers

FOR PROFESSIONALS:

Getting to Yes: Negotiating Agreement Without Giving In. Second or Third Edition.
Fisher, R.., Ury, W., & Patton, B. (2011, 1991, 1983, 1981). New York: Penguin Books.
Getting Past No: Negotiating in Difficult Situations
Ury, W. (1993, 1991). New York: Penguin Books.
The Guided Method of Mediation: A Return to the Original Ideals of ADR. Second Edition
Hope, M.K., (2014a; 2009). Raleigh, NC: Pax Pugna Publishing
Mediating Interpersonal Conflicts: A Pathway to Peace
Umbreit, M. (2006, 1995). Wipf & Stock Publishers
Pastoral Mediation: An Innovative Practice. Second Edition
Hope, M. K., (2014b; 2009). Raleigh, NC: Pax Pugna Publishing
Practitioner Heal Thyself: Challenges in Enabling Organizational Health. **(2004). Kathryn Goldman Schuyler**
Organization Management Journal. Emerging Scholarship. 2004. Vol. 1. No. 1. Pp. 28-37.

The Skilled Facilitator: A Comprehensive Resource for Consultants, Facilitators, Managers, Trainers and Coaches
Schwarz, R. (2002; 1994). San Francisco: Jossey-Bass

Role-Plays for Resolution. Second Edition
Hope, M. K., (2014c; 2010). Raleigh, NC: Pax Pugna Publishing
The P.A.C.E. Method: Conflict Resolution for First Responders:
Hope, M.K. (2014d). Raleigh, NC: Pax Pugna Publishing.
Transcending Cycles of Violence: The RING of Conflict Resolution
Hope, M.K. (2014e). Raleigh, NC: Pax Pugna Publish

Negotiate Journal™

I. Here is What I Want To Happen:

_____
_____
_____
_____
_____

I. What I Need:

_____
_____
_____
_____
_____

II. What Does **The Other Side** Want To Happen?

_____
_____
_____
_____

II. What Does **The Other Side** Need?

_____
_____
_____
_____

Be true to how YOU would really feel if YOU were experiencing what THEY are.
Do you know exactly what they are going through? <u>Take Time to Find Out How They Feel</u>.

NOW compare your **want** sheets with your opponent's **want** sheets.

THEN Compare your **need** sheets with your opponent's **need** sheets.

Page 1   © Mary Kendall Hope

Negotiate Journal™

List Any Similar WANTS: **List Any Similar NEEDS:**

III.   SAME WANTS   SAME NEEDS

1._____   1._____
2._____   2._____
3._____   3._____
4._____   4._____
5._____   5._____
_____
_____
_____

Now Read these lists and take some time to think.

IV.   **Create Some New Statements in your thinking based on**
What You've Written Down.

1._____
2._____
3._____
4._____
5._____
6._____
7._____

V.   **What *Statements of Respect* Can You Use to Request**
What You Want to Happen?

1._____
2._____
3._____

What *Statements of Respect* Can You Use to Request
What You Need:

1._____
2._____

Made in the USA
Columbia, SC
28 August 2017